Poetic Perspectives

Edited by Sarah Worley

poetrynow

First published in Great Britain in 2005 by:
Poetry Now
Remus House
Coltsfoot Drive
Peterborough
PE2 9JX
Telephone: 01733 898101
Website: www.forwardpress.co.uk

SB ISBN 1 84602 030 1

Foreword

Although we are a nation of poets we are accused of not reading poetry, or buying poetry books. After many years of listening to the incessant gripes of poetry publishers, I can only assume that the books they publish, in general, are books that most people do not want to read.

Poetry should not be obscure, introverted, and as cryptic as a crossword puzzle: it is the poet's duty to reach out and embrace the world.

The world owes the poet nothing and we should not be expected to dig and delve into a rambling discourse searching for some inner meaning.

The reason we write poetry (and almost all of us do) is because we want to communicate: an ideal; an idea; or a specific feeling. Poetry is as essential in communication, as a letter; a radio; a telephone, and the main criterion for selecting the poems in this anthology is very simple: they communicate.

Contents

The Poems

Gift Of The Holy Spirit

Blessed spirit
Earth's gift from the Father and the Son;
Intercessor, the key which unlocks the door
From Earth to Heaven,
Hear our prayers.
Comforter, be there, the unseen presence when we call.
In sickness, in grief, in despair.
Turn the hearts of evil men,
Influence and change the greedy for power,
the uncaring destroyer,
with your mighty cleansing wind.
Ignite the world with tongues of flame;
tongues that unite the universe
in one voice of peace and unity . . .
so that all may join the praise of the Trinity,
three in one, one in three,
Father, Son and Holy Spirit,
Ever present,
Ever constant
Everlasting
Amen.

Di Bagshawe

Frog In A Pondweed Hat

The pale glow of the morning sun drips over the knotwork
of branches,
to dapple liquid gold upon the opaque green, shadowing the
pond's surface.
A gentle whisper in the wind lifts a veil of translucent leaves,
casts away the shadow to hint at amber pebbles on the bank.

Out of the silent water thrust water lilies,
their leathery leaves poised for the first burst of light.
It comes and fractures the surface into white glass.
A water lily bud slowly flickers into life.
Each petal unravels to reveal a flame of vivid pink.

Frogs protrude their faces from underneath the glittering surface.
Stillness is disrupted with a splash.
A frog leaping into the calmness,
casting a shower of sparkling beads that ripple the surface,
surging water boatmen into life, diving into the emerald weed.

A frog, now looking at me, wearing a pondweed hat sits still
and waits.
Unsuspecting flies hover, a snake in the grass watches.
I drink my tea and watch the world in the sunlight.

Sigurd Ramans Harborough

Blood-Red

Blood-Red, Blood-Red,
Silently falling from on high in the Albert Hall
The service people standing tall.
The elderly, still marching in time to the band
- After all these years they can barely stand.
Salute them.
Now new widows whose loved ones were so very young,
Never had chance to march in step
But officials, complete with band, gave
Them a funeral, very grand.
Blood-Red, Blood-Red.
They died because they obeyed.
As we throw away the peace, they must feel betrayed.
They died that we might learn
But we go back to war at the slightest turn.
Salute them and *listen*.
Don't just listen to them politely, listen to them and learn.
Hold their experience tightly. Don't ever forget and stand firm.
Instil in your hearts never to take part in killing.
Refuse to be dragged into war.
It's an insult to those who have saved us
And never came home to our shore.
Blood Red. Blood Red.
Poppies silently fall and cover the floor
In the Albert Hall.

J W Whiteacre

Late Summer In St George's Park

Save for swans
I have the place to myself
What bliss!

A late summer Saturday
With English football heroes
On the field of battle?

Or something.
Or somewhere.

Solitude is ensured

Affording an opportunity of thought
In Wandsworth.

St George's Park.

D Ross

Natural Disaster

Well will you look
For God's sake,
How does she manage that . . .
If anyone sees or hears - dear God,
They'll think me such a prat.

She listens to rock, Bruce Willis DVD.
If I walk very quickly, she may not see me.

She used to be so lovely,
There *was* potential there.
(But she knows what I've forgotten, to her I'm laid bare)

I'll see her again when I have time,
She wouldn't fit in here.
When I try to improve her she never speaks,
Her fingers fumble with fear.

She couldn't cope in my kind of life,
A lamb to the slaughter,
No really, as she walks away,
You'd never think her my daughter . . .

Emma Eliott

God's Gift

How wonderful this world of ours
God's gift to humanity
The changing of the seasons
From darkness, to the light of day

The beauty of the flowers
And fields of green
The richness of the golden corn
Ripened by the hot summer sun

Blue skies above as
Pure white clouds drift along
Coloured rays of sunshine
Sparkles on the sea
Forming shimmering diamonds
A glorious sight to see

Large trees in the forest
A deep smell of pine
Every flower has its own perfume
Toxicating on a gentle breeze

Storms rage, and strong winds blow
Ebb and flowing tides
Ice-caped mountains of snow
Earthquakes made to destroy
These gifts God gave us
For a little while to enjoy.

Doreen Petherick Cox

The Seagull

Am I the seagull flying high
swooping, soaring against a blue
and cloud-patched sky?
Feathered form of blinding white,
each shaft caught in storm bright light.
Early morning walk along river's edge,
of a June and summer day.

Leaning over embankment
rough rasp of wall hard beneath
and waters dank, green depths below.
A placid calm of mud-flat brown,
where ducks preen lazily among puddles wet,
as low tide waits for full moon's night
of a June and summer day.

Seagull turns, and eye-to-eye
the stare we share. Taut in time,
no time: 'all'. Unite as one in 'being'.
Am I the seagull or the seagull I?
Under that blue and storm cast sky,
of a June and summer day.
I and seagull: Seagull and I.

A D M Thomas

The Scratching Of A Pen

I always knew you'd stay strong,
When I left your side.
You carried on with your fractured life.

The sweet smell of honey radiating from the larder.
And the morning dewdrops,
Still clinging to the lady's mantle I gave you,
On your 18th birthday.
Simple memories of me.

I look back at the old clarinet
Lying broken, in pieces on the kitchen floor.
Reflecting the psalm of a broken heart,
Your broken heart.

Memories of us together, forever grip
The scent of freshly washed laundry.
That I helped you with so many times,
When your washer stopped spinning.

Although my life has stopped spinning,
Yours will not stop unfolding.
Keep the letters wrapped up in red velvet,
As I sing you a melody down from the heavens.

You look back to this old book,
By a poor poet's hand
And see the ink stains running,
Intertwined with my tears.
Our song comes on the radio,
'Truly, Madly, Deeply' you sigh.

A wet page, freshly salted.
Masked by the sounds of a gentle breeze.
And the scratching of a pen.

Lucy Kolaj

Portrait Of R S Thomas

It is your eyes, firstly; tired
And weary they rest upon life
The same way they rest
On your congregation. You stand,
A face between God
And Man, Jones, Williams, Thomas, Evans -
Attempt to search the harsh contours
Of your face
For signs of an Almighty presence; tracing
The tracks of time, weighted
By candelight perhaps
You convey the small details
Of life onto your page. And with your talk
Of bread and wine, you offer insight unseen
From the spaces
Between the words.
As if spindrift collected
In a silent fury
Upon the sea, your unspoken sermon
Gathers a rich harvest of pale flesh
As the ruthless breath of many winters
Blush the faces of those in the pews.

Andrèa Davies

At The Crossroads

I should have stopped and asked the way,
instead I walked over the same crossroads
several times, back and forth I would go,
as silly as it may seem I was lost!

Trouble is, I was stubborn enough to
think I was on the right road.
It took me some time but eventually,
I had to admit to myself,
That I was hopelessly lost.

It's a simple question to ask!
But, if you're not sure where you are going;
How can you know the way?

It's a simple question, and a vital accepting,
If you want to go to Heaven.
Only God's word can lead the way.

Heavenly Father, I pray,
Please show me how to love You every single day,
and forgive me my stubbornness,
when I am lost and gone astray.
Teach me by Your word each and every day.

Heavenly Father,
in Your mercy,
please show me Your way,
In Jesus name I ask, In Jesus name I pray,
Amen.

Robert Waggitt

Out Of Eden

I had a dream
Of ageless Eden,

A breath of true life
From a garden forbidden.

For I was an outcast
A slave newborn.

A crying wife
My thistle and thorn.

It was so wrong to eat
Of the fruit of the tree,

Now the knowledge of good
And evil's in me . . . but . . .

As I walk the Earth
No worse than some,

Others tell me, that
'Jesus has come' . . .

Now I have new knowledge,
Now I can see,

A crossroad to Heaven
Provided for me.

Roger Mosedale

Respect A Woman's Consent

A kiss is a kiss and will never be sex.
Romance is romance and will never be sex.
Flirting is just flirting and is not at all sex.
Ask for it politely and you will be given.
Where there is a *will* there is a *way*.

Never trespass someone's private property.
Never impose yourself on someone's thongs
Impose yourself and you will be jailed
Hey you lustful bloke respect a woman's consent
And avoid jail. Respect her consent and
Enjoy every minute of it.

Thomas Mutangiri

Reach Out And Touch

Reach out and touch, do not fear
Reach out and touch, the Lord is near
So near is Our Lord, He is within us
Christ our living Lord
Christ our living Lord, let me Thy servant be
Make me an example of Your Christ-like love
Then by Thy grace in serving Thee I serve all.
Christ who suffered and died for all
Help me to see Thee in broken humanity
Those who suffer in whatever way
Let me in Your name
Reach out, touch and love and in doing so
May they feel comforted and drawn closer to Thee
O Christ our living Lord
Through all Your suffering and pain
You died and rose again, that we may live,
In the hope of joining You in the great Eternity.
Where You will reach out and touch us
And draw us into the heart of Your eternal love.

M Cubis

The Thin Man

A man I know
said to me
make me an omelette
cooked flat in a frying pan,
it started with one egg,
and now it's up to three,
to eat before his dinner.

He thinks about food
all the time
by now he should be
getting big and bigger
but that isn't so,
instead he is getting thin and thinner.

I've had to put a chain
around the fridge
to stop him snacking
all through the day.

No wondering where the food has gone!
It's gone inside me.

Anita Shedlow

Veni Veni Emmanuel

Another dawn will never break for them,
Veni Veni Emmanuel.
Their day is over without their knowing,
Veni Veni Emmanuel.
Their panic and destruction is our legacy,
The memory will not fade away.

But light must shine from the face of despair,
Veni Veni Emmanuel.
Love must come with a world that comes together in grief.
Veni Veni Emmanuel.
We may not understand or ever know the reason why,
There may be no reason, while our hearts remain sad.

Bring us together, let us work for peace,
Veni Veni Emmanuel.
Let us work together to bring light out of darkness,
Veni Veni Emmanuel.
Let us never forget this horror that lies before us,
But allow us to unite in a massive push towards a world in one,
Veni Veni Emmanuel.
Amen.

John Cook

The Rainbow People

Who are these people
and what does it mean?
They are the children of god
for they shall inherit the Earth.
Like Noah before them
they shall have peace.

For many a good Christian
shall become a peacemaker of our time.
For they shall see their god when it's time.
Pure and holy is this the right time.

Kate Davies

Fish Tank In The Corner

There's a fish tank in the lobby
With tropical fish inside
It used to be a hobby of mine
It used to give me pride

Now I have a satellite dish!
And the tank is bare
For, you see it's very clear
There are no fish in there!

All the fish are now outside
Gawping, ogle-eyed
At the gibberish on the screen
It makes me want to hide.

S Farley

Pale Memory

Gravely, I stand
on a windswept cliff;
chilled to the bone
under an empty sky.
I gaze along
a gravel path,
which meanders
towards the beach.
where the mists of time
roll backwards
to a pale memory
of summer's glow.

I remember the sound
of my last breath,
taken on a
dreamless day.
It echoes
on the cliff-top breeze.
And in a heartbeat
I am swept away,
knowing that tomorrow
I shall return again
to haunt this place
once more.

M M Graham

My Mothers

I was raised by my grandmothers, aunts, sisters, stepmum and Mum.
In my job and in my life, I have met so many wonderful women
Even tho' I am not related to them, yet they treat me just like
a daughter.
Their love is so infectious and knows no bound.
Their words of encouragement are so sweet and juicy.
Their support is like the rock of Gibraltar.
Lean on me when you are happy or sad.
Trust me as I believe in you.
To my mothers on the Earth plane and in spirit world.
I love you all with all my soul.
May you always be surrounded in God's love and light.
You see! I cannot even write this poem without Your love.
I learnt from the best.
Luckyyyyy meee!
Sending you all a rainbow of hope, love and kisses.

O Oshinbolu

A Friend Remembered

Active and young, you moved and learned
with speed, following each fresh track
as far as it could lead,
at times alone,
sometimes with ring of friends,
growing with them as the years matured.
Now, like a ripe fruit fallen,
suddenly you're dead!

You gave some warning, I now see,
and felt the way ahead,
but great the shock and sad the space
now - suddenly, you're dead!

On my last visit, sharing tea and talk,
we looked out of the window
at the flowering garden,
and on the walls, admired in detail
the pictures from your family and friends.
Some I knew and some were names
of those I never met
but heard of through the years
our friendship lasted.
They became imagined people
in my circle, just as you lived
part of mine with those you never met.
That upstairs room welcomed with tea and talk
so many times, and often reappears
in dreams, a special atmosphere
of half-discovered places just beyond
that will remain mysterious.
Three meetings in one week brought us together,
next day, suddenly, you died.
Photos, memories, dreams, are partial pictures
But - you're dead!

Ruth Partington

The Resurrection

A bloodied cross
Was dismantled
Upon the ground
Of Golgotha,
Drying in the
Death-stenched air.
Fragrant linens
Encased scorged flesh
But for a moment . . .

Blinding light
Revealed blood-soaked
Linens discarded in a
Rich man's tomb.
As foretold,
On the third day,
He had arisen,
He was raised
By resurrection power
To receive His reward;
The nations of this world,
And the glory of
His matchless name.

Alice Parris

Quietly In Chapel

The invisibility of your presence
is forever here,
The smell of the flowers
caught on floating air,
The prayer book
guiding your unconditional love,
The bible
and the witnessed miracles of God
who taught us to forgive,
and left his legacy of love eternal,
Shall we sit quite still
and simply worship him?

Margarette Phillips

Fractured Dreams

Dreams fractured,
I sleep in constant dread
palm-pressing my bruised limbs.

A part of me paralysed,
I slump into my shroud
force-fed by the other half
to stay alive.

Light breaks out
from the shrapnel gloom
and I slog through mire
in search of elixir.

How empty sound
the vows of peace
after every war,
how hollow the victory claims!

The earth mined,
no spot for a sapling of peace,
the stench sickening;
all down the drain.

Madan Gandhi

Black

it's dark in here, let me out.
nobody can hear me shout.
it's so cold, i'm all alone.
the darkness seeping into my bones.

the silence. screaming in my ears.
the shadows feeding on my fears.
they're hiding. where, i cannot see.
my demons out to feast on me.

nowhere to run. nowhere to hide.
my heart. a stone. lies still inside.
my soul fades. time passes by.
the final dance of a butterfly.

Kirsty Koeswoyo

Trapped - Compacted Opposition

Imprisoned in an abandoned mind, down into an
unoccupied tranquillity.
To imply reality is to be invisibly immersed in a distant silhouette,
Resembling an obscure dominant agony
The perfect destination - untouchable as seeing the fragility
of indifference dissolved
Like an unextinguished taper, inevitably vanishing into an
immaculate death
Purified by fire into a recognizable dust
It is unbearable to witness the continuous imaginations that
incessantly awaken
Repeating that identified transparency inlaid into the wound
To banish into nothingness in an instant
To separate into a new direction, revealed yet unspeakable
But it is all a mirrored illusion - reflecting endlessly
The imminent consequence guarded beneath a sensitive
reorganisation
To divert and refine that incessant, perceived agony.

Hilary Jean Clark

To Try, And Fail

Why do I love you?
You drown my soul in so much woe
I am a moth to the flame
Tempted by false light
The light is my friend
The fire is my home

I stand by you
Though it is so hard
But the thought you may leave me
Tears at my skin
Grips at my heart

So like a fool
I absorb your pain
Like it is my own

I could try and teach you
To be better
Stronger
Trust again
But I feel my life will be over
To look back
There will be no faith
No love that remains.

Bryony Freeman

Curium

I was a painted urn, I was a ball and chain.
I was lost in a whirl of seraphim sand.
Straight-armed I swam through the churning
Sea, all in a fall towards you - who lay
Unaware, fevering through a dream.

Alexander Lowell

Broken Wings

What a waste. Was that it?
Where did I go wrong on this long journey?
A husband I hated, children just wasted,
In this world so overrated.
Could I relive it, never to fill it
With all of the misery?
Life is a mystery. Let this be history.
God help me.

Barbara Brannelly

Stardust

. . . I behold upon the night's starred face,
Huge cloudy symbols of a high romance . . .
John Keats (1795-1821)

Brave young eagle with painful broken wing,
What was the object of your cruel sickness?
Just to stop in time your early flight in
Ways and lines of grace? And yet you scanned well
The strange mystery of Spenser's moonbeams.

Your cloudy symbols once again will speak.
But now our feet must still be on the ground.
And time must wait for souls to grub with noses
Low to hunt throughout the wood until we
May emerge and see the whole once more.

But no, the magic of your hand was not
By chance. For these same stars will shortly tell
Necessity's long tale. But not of woe
As we go tomorrow through this summer's
Madness not to fresh woods but pastures new.

You did not mourn alone. Nor yet again
Were you dispersed in passing nebulae
As dust. But we must wait at this full stop.
The bus will come along and when it does
They'll know again the meaning of romance.

Desmond Tarrant

Words Like A Waterfall

Letters falling over the edge,
Tumbling, cascading, into the maelstrom below.
Sinking then swirling,
Each letter with a magnetic pull to another
To gel into chains.

The problem is getting the right order,
To go into the mind, to convey the feeling,
That the words can give.
To those that wish to see.

Some letters have an affinity,
To express the correct thought like magnetism,
Other letters will float onwards,
And down to the sea.
Ready to recycle,
And try all over again.

Barry Kendall

Blue In The Silence

A true friend is for life,
Though yours was shorter,
The day we met, I knew you'd be mine
I handed over the money,
You were divine.
Those big brown eyes,
Showed emotion, you couldn't speak -
At least not to me.
But in you I found a great friend
One I could talk to, never end.
You never answered me back,
But nudged me with your muzzle
As if to say 'don't be down'
You looked after me
Just as I did you
A mutual understanding - silence between us.
Never patronising, rude or frowning
For hours in the night
You let me share your stable,
Time well spent
For now you are no longer here
A very sad loss,
But I will never forget
Those nights together of warm silence.
Your stable now empty
I sit here alone - cold in the silence
Wishing I could have you back.

Mandy Preston

Live Clean

Soft sweet smile; open face; will she fall from grace?
Impish adolescent youth' will he become the man?
Pitfalls for too many! Background, breeding, do they count?
A needle's not what life's about: but living cleanly is!

Deception runs a gauntlet to an all suspicious eye,
It's done with lies, breaks human ties, heartache closely by.
What's now gone today; was seen here yesterday!
Failings by the wayside; respect no longer there.

To dwell within one's anguish now, an eye detects a lie.
We live with hope it's not that dope; leads one on to die.
That job no longer there, makes raised senses more aware,
Some risk death with solvents; ignoring caption care.

Why take a chance of soaring high, to self-destruct below?
Where peaks cannot be reached, come that fatal flaw!
When selfishness is mixed with greed, and consequences blind.
More lives than one may finish: think those then left behind!

David Pooley

Look In A Mirror And Stare At A Blank Page

How can you sit
And judge me so easily?
Presume you know what is best
And all the flaws of my intellect?
Only I know my true worth
So let me explain it to you.

My life is a blank piece of paper
It is getting smaller every day
Its blankness, not void,
But room for potential and creativity.
Only I know the direction the lines flow,
Unlike others, no one writes life for me.

My mind is like a pen, full of ink
So much, it can be added to, and never runs out.
With this I could be like anyone
And write something dull and meaningless,
Or I could write something never before said
And find the solution to a thousand problems.

I will use every scrap of life to create
I don't want to spend life copying up.
I know the strength of my mind
I will create and become something great
So trust my ambition and intuition.
Don't try and read into what hasn't been written.

Duncan Catterall

Cradle To Grave

From the cradle to the grave
We have this bond
A bond that nothing can touch
You don't have to be with you
To know
The unconditional door
Is always open
Even after life, your presence is there
And is of comfort.

Any problems, any tears we shed
It's you we want
Nobody kisses it better
Than Mum does

On this day
More than any other
I want you to know
The love I have is yours
Now and forever

Thank you
For being wonderful
For being you.

Rachael Cowham

Nascence

In the broad sweep of the day it is
soul I seek, and soul is my idol and aim.
Soul, in perception, is found in twilight.
In a movement and a light of
if not grace then grace mixed with clay,
yet I see and love it in twilight.

That grace should touch us is a speeding train -
it brings to us gifts from Heaven.
That grace should mix with clay is the
sensuous part of Heaven come to mix with us -
In love of purity God is pouring forth His grace
to mix with stained flesh and make soul.

Paul Barron

The Door

Go and open the door.
Maybe there's a wolf that dances,
Or a lion that knows his A, B, C.
Or a cup that can read seven books at the same time.

Go and open the door.
Maybe there's a dog that can sing.
Or a dictionary that can speak
Or a comb that says, 'No I will do it.'

Go and open the door.
Maybe there's a jug that can do a back-flip.
Or a cat that can play a game in a minute.
Or a bag that goes, 'Ho, oh, hi.'

Go and open the door.
Maybe there's a kiss that goes far.
Or a care bear that knows how to give a good time.
Or a dinosaur that knows everything.
Come on open the door.

Courtney Woodhead (9)

A Moment Of Time

Here, neither fluctuating nor deviating, yet intent on relinquishing to
your future spasm of time.
A moment of truth, a moment of lie, a moment of love or one of hate.
Neither intruding on our will nor extinguishing our thought, yet here for
us to use for good or ill.
Aware of your awesome presence, yet you escape and then the next,
never to be experienced in a lifetime again.
How were you used you moment of a moment ago?
How tiny you seem, but yet how overpoweringly awe-inspiring.
How quiet you are in stillness but where can we find you in the
tumultuous cacophony of sound?
With how much respect are you treated in a world so frighteningly
Divesting herself of such a necessary commodity?
To kill or heal, to maim or bless?
You moment of a life, do you feel sadness or joy or are you
just here?
Neither taking from the last nor giving to the next, you exist uniquely
embodied in a terrible power.
Are you the last moment of my time?
Do you know how many of you are allotted to me?
Do you know when to stop for me?
Unlike the butterfly caught in the net you are free, never to
be trapped.
You moment of ecstasy or joy, grief or pain you flee, gone forever.
You moment of a moment ago to whom do you flee?
Where is your home?
Where do you go?
You moment of time, your existence is shrouded in veils of mystery,
How beautiful, how terrifying, how sure.
Friend or foe, or are you just here touch-typing the clouds in the
valleys of space as we dream on, some of us searching and wishing
for more of your sweetness, others eager, to bid you farewell.

Catherine O'Halloran

Evening Sky

Above the rushing silvered rills
that to summer rains vivify,
mountains bare their jagged
teeth and square their shoulders
to the sky.
Spirits of the wind through slopes
of sombre pines cascade their
leafy chatter;
stars, the dreams of men and tall
ships the night skies flatter.
Gilded to their evening light
quiet hills keep silent vigil,
O'er a landscape bathed in
moonlight, at peace and tranquil.

Peter Morriss

Grandfather's Door

The wooden staircase spirals,
Narrowing with every tread. It climbs
Ever upwards, a journey back in time.
I touch the door,
Rich with the patina of age.
Reflecting an earlier pride in beauty.
Glowing wood,
Burnished brass,
Glistening glass,
A doorway to my childhood.

Through the door, his workshop
Scarcely the size of a cave. And yet
Full of his treasures. The tools of his trade
Gathered together,
Serving his skilful hand.
On his bench lies a rainbow of leather,
Punches and knives.
Needles of steel,
Thread on a reel,
A magical place when you're five.

The smell of brand new leather,
Wraps round me like a cloak, I'm safe
And welcome, in this special place.
Grandfather at his bench.
Day upon day, year upon year,
Every last stitch created with care,
Needle spears,
Left hand and right,
All this despite
His four times-twenty years.

Margaret Crossland

The Word 'Nuclear'

It's all in the word!

If it hadn't been for
    Hiroshima
        and Nagasaki
would 'nuclear'
    just be a type of power station?

If it hadn't been for
    Catholic
        and Protestant;
hatred, torture and killings;
would 'Christianity'
    just be another religion?

If it hadn't been for
    the 'Twin Towers';
now the hatred and killings . . .

what will the word 'Islam'
    become?

B Sommer

Coming Home

Come home.
Come home to me -
I left the door ajar
to see you coming
from afar -
a tired bard.

The night is heavy.
The way is hard.

And yet you will,
for things have to follow their track -
It has been written
in the stars
that our souls move intact.

Lucina Zayder

Survive

A net to make - a spider's job,
Failed again and again.
But never we hear his sob,
Well done, true man.

A dream awoke from a beach,
Entering into the sea of life.
For the seashore beyond to reach,
Going through every storm.

A horse is galloping with hope,
Over mountains, over meadows -
Steps never stop without a rope,
With pride, raising its nose.

A sound never stops asking, 'Why
Is life rough as a sea, hard to dive?'
Another sound answers, 'Never say die!
People who are bold will survive.'

Haiying Zhang

Your Smile

(Dedicated to a girl who works at my gym)

You are so alive
With beauty so bright
I see the sun in your eyes
Every time you smile
It's such a beautiful sight
The way you light up the room
Your smile, I love it
It's beauty so poetic
I like to see your smile shine
So never let it fade
As I say in closing
I love your smile
Once again.

Matthew Holloway

Hidden In The Shadows

Hidden in the angular shadows
He edges forward toward his victim
Slowly, slowly creeping forward
Without making a noise he slowly descends

She stands at the mirror, brushing her hair
Once, twice, three times, brushing
Unaware of the oncoming terror
The terror that lies just beyond the light

He slows his descent and watches
She turns from the mirror, reaches for the light switch
He pounces. He lands. She screams.
The spider scurries away, smiling at his triumph.

Elizabeth Brindley

Call Us What You Like

We may be fat, thin, ugly, disabled
or into writing poems and making blankets,
but we know who we are
and what we like doing,
but we know that deep down inside
our hearts we are just ourselves
we don't need to hide away
from these bullies, we
should stand up to them
and make them see we ain't
scared of them.

Amanda Prince

Hiatus

Seize time from that which incarcerates each second
Minute by minute. Hour by hour. Day by day.
The circean cacophony of the city
Dictates
Syncopated only by humanity.
Frame a door in the frenzy of consciousness
Emergency exit this way!
Fling it wide but walk through without haste
Out from the ceaseless ebb and flow
The circadian rhythms.
Such a small step
To escape the machinations of life
Listen. Feel.
The automaton within now without

J F Murfitt

Ecstasy Of An End

The passion of grief has an extra depth,
A seething cup of need;
And after the initial waiting for cue,
It burrows in to feed.
Painless as it enters, unnoticed by the parts that lied,
And as it impatiently burns inside it's banished from outside.

Paranoid paralysis, emotion engulfing pow'r,
The before buried to cool its fire was once a blooming flower,
Now awaiting final judgement in limbo locked away
Until release, good or bad, on that welcome final day.

Keys issued in the hour unlock the stiff, bound tears,
Allowing the release of need and the beauty of our fears,
An end to rest from coping, fight over whether lost or won,
Ecstasy of an end to lies of faces brightly shone.

Darkness quiet and daylight gone.
But home.

Denise Delaney

Love In Blackpool

Day is done on the Front.
The slim back-street unpacked
from ram-jam loops of daytime cars.
Rita bears the brunt
of punters' leery barmaid cracks
In The Public Bar. In her Stars.

There has to be a gangling lover
bearing down: police undercover?
Pierce Brosnan? Freelance darts pro
muscles a-go-go, fertile as vitro?

She trembles. He comes:
an asthmatic son of Man,
trash-man Ron, hair limp dangling,
waddling wobbly turns,
cuddling a Heineken can,
probing a Doritos bag, ambling.

She flicks a lip-glossed fag away
on an unmanned Lunar flight, leasing
herself to earthly folds, the squiffy clay
of a drinking man, and love increasing

beyond the Back Sunday.
A craven car will shoot out
clandestine, breaking Love
off the agenda, so sweetly drawn.
Tumbling sky, grey will cover.
Mute, strong Manxmen will rub hands with phlegm,

Cloning beery tears on the dancing breeze.
In the lee of debris pushed up on the shore
The ghost head rocks will stay, unexcorcised,
Even in the sweat of the summer saloon.

We die, die, die, so soon, so soon, and must be forgotten;
yet, as pints thud on the sodden bar-room tray,
the mute men yell for the sake of company.
Rita and Ron have pried their laid-back way
from cemetery to pub: loved still, still prized,
still in love.

Philip Burton

Chrysalis

Look all around you
See what I see
Try to imagine
Just how I feel
Every little thing
Holds beauty inside
It's not always obvious
With patience it hides
You may not believe it
But sweetheart it's true
That self same beauty
Hides deep within you
You live and breathe now
Like a flower shut tight
Or a chrysalis spun
On warm summer night
But know time will help
Make you see what is real
You'll grow and mature
And one day reveal
That childishness past
A young woman now grown
You'll look in the mirror
One day and will own
That finally, suddenly
No hint of warning
A butterfly's beauty
Within you was growing.

Linda Howitt

Knight In Armour

Your kiss is like the summer rain
As it slowly caresses my face
Your touch is like the warmth of the wind
As it glides across my skin
Your smell is like a mystery
Just waiting to be solved
You've wrapped me in your warm embrace
To protect, and to love
You've given me a reason
For a future in the stars
You've given me a season
To remember when times are hard
You've taken me in your arms
And held me oh so tight
And for this my knight in armour
I give you my love.

Sherri Dubyts

My Inadequacy

Down by seafront some mentally handicapped people
Were enjoying their selves.
They were a little noisy
They were talking, demonstrating
What they wanted because of their disabilities,
In language they knew.

They had with them two happy carers
Who I envied in their way, because
They understood, keeping their
Charges happy people, looking after them,
This time now part of my day.

Me, I felt a little awkward as people all sat very nearby,
Not unpleasant just uncomfortable,
But it was something I was unprepared for,
So in many an instance, I kept my gaze averted
In case by my looking they involved me.

These folk were not at fault
They being natural in their world,
It was me who could not see.
They were communicating best way they could,
It was I in my ignorance never understood.

Well I brought my gaze around to face them,
One man mentally handicapped in a wheelchair,
Looked at me, smiled, I said, 'Hello,'
Smiled back, he seemed pleased,
Tapped his chest, I knew I had made effort
To knock my silly inadequacy down,
I felt better too.

Victoria Joan Theedam

Mountain Top

I have seen a wondrous sight,
I have had a wondrous night.
Perched upon a mountain top.
I had thought I had seen
Quite a lot.
And now I sit upon a rock.
Upon this
Majestic mountain top.
The wind has come up,
The temperature has dropped.
Cold and peaceful,
Deadly and harsh,
The snow has closed the only pass.
When winter has gone
And there is a spring thaw.
I think I will come back,
Just to walk some more.
But now I am off
Sliding away, I am skiing you see,
On this cold beautiful day.

K Cook

Behind Closed Doors

When he locks the door
I know it is time.
No longer do I act afraid
my body has become
accustomed to his touch.
Unlike before
when his flesh made mine crawl,
now it just makes me numb.
He now chooses not to reassure me
that he still loves me,
we both know he does not
and the threats of retribution
if I tell, have all but ceased.
I only wish my life
would as well.

Ian Benjamin

Oh Dear!

She's a perfectly dreadful woman
The woman who came to stay;
She looked after my dogs and my house
As merry I went on my way.

She cleaned out my father's garden
And dug up the fishpond too;
Three days the fishes swam in his sink
Whilst she bleached their home shiny new.

Now they swim in a sanitised pool
Too scared to glub out their fears;
That Domestos ain't no good for them
Just makes them swim in top gear!

When I went on a trip to Glasgow
She laid waste my flowerbed;
Gave to the neighbours my daffy bulbs
And threw away plants that looked dead.

But dead they were most certainly not
Just resting until next year;
She always tries to take over
Oh why did she have to come here?

She put out forty bags of refuse
Another eight's still to go;
The scaffy man's lorry was laden,
'She's obsessed!' was his cry of woe.

'Why on earth do I have her?' you say
Well, habits die hard I guess;
The dogs love her, she spoils them you see
And the house has no muddles or mess.

When hubby dies she's got it all planned
She's coming down here to live;
A cottage she'll buy, a garden she'll make
But I'll have no flowers to give!

Joanne Burns

Candle In The Chapel

On these grounds I am a beggar: not begging for food
but to give you my heart, I lift my head like a flower,
search for words; emotion unsteadies me as I take myself
into the light so I might caress you when you look.

You turn your back to me and I burn, do not utter a word,
make your shadow visible as it follows the procession:
all leave through the same door.
And I learn to be happy in the flow of my tears.
I arch like you till my cry melts with the others,
gather body for my light. Love betters it with fire.
I'm a beggar in this land, so rich.

Elena Tincu-Straton

Untitled

The great city of London is so busy
Within the fizzy weather
And there never is any room to move a broom
For the tramps to feed the rats
Without seeing any of the pussy cats
To give them clean showers
So they can be awarded the smells from their violets
And pilots who know all the blossoms beneath the tower bridges
When all the London rascals are having sleeps inside these
iceberg fridges
Which provides all the permissions for the Crown Court Judges
to leave their castles
With their wonder pigs on leads to walk down the high streets
Helping their masters to choose some extra bright pink wigs
So they can see their reflections coming up from the pavements
While filling their cement mixers up with the rat races
So they can make clear space when doing their shoelaces into
the double bows
While watching their arrows making the right ways to
the roundabouts
Where all the larger louts are shouting at each other
While making daisy chains for each other
So hopefully one sun ray day
They will find a lover on a London Sunday.

Steven Pearson

Daddy

It has been a long time since you were a giant to me;
Since I cowered beneath the weight of your presence.
In many drawn out nights of sleeplessness.
As shadows smudge my eyes like long distant memories of you,
I carefully fill the holes that you left in my confidence
with solid building blocks of hatred.

I imagine meeting you again now, our conversation would be brief
I would begin:
'No'

I would not need to say more
because in this one forbidden word I have lain down my challenge
and my revenge.
For if you still believe that I will be small
beneath your thunderous advance,
if you think I will still fall meek to my knees
as you blacken my eyes
and paint my skin with the violent darkness of your rage,
then you have not grown up so much in all your years
as I have since you left.

Suie Nettle

Archaic Methods

Increasingly, all the way through the
Unified line, the saltmarsh furrow is constructed,
All the way through over the plain, persistently
Guidelines are kept to, single constructions
Still from the high trig points, above.

Michael Soper

The Light Switch At The Corridor's End

The blackness appears hostile
Eternal in its cold and desolate anger
Silently striking fear into your heart.
Facing it alone
An icy trickle of sweat gathers on your brow
What now?
Do you advance or retreat?
Or wait for the morning light to come!

Hated from early days of childhood
The darkness of the night was never your friend
It was despised, feared and phobic
Screams would not dissolve the inky void then
A scream will not resolve the situation now,
Courage is needed
Nerves of steel
A heroic task
To thwart the unseen danger within.

As you survey what you cannot see
Imagination runs out of control,
Did something move, was there a sound?
What dreaded phantom awaits
To gentle touch you as you pass
And frighten you to Hell!

In your mind you know there is nothing there
So you make your move,
Swiftly, you dash to the far away wall
And switch on the light of life.

George S Johnstone

Fruit Of Worldly Love

The fruit of worldly love, ripened, sweetened then its juice turned
to wine
It intoxicated, confused and filled my mind
I stumbled in a stupor, and ignored so much more
My head was filled with hallucinations of passion, of meanings and
drunken understandings.
There was joy and celebration as I lay puking on the floor
That wine runs dry and winds my mind around its empty flask.
I want so much to find a drunkenness that lasts
So I turn to an unworldly fruit, an ecstasy that endures.
I drink the wine of divine grapes, always sweet, with no morning
after pain.
The figments of its fermentation are real and firm.
This bottle never empties
I sing drunkard's songs, lost within the verse, wandering the Earth.

Should we ever meet, I will offer you a drink.

Chrystine Julian

Winter's Last Stand

The sun shone down from skies of blue.
It seemed that Spring was on her way,
The birds began to sing.
Snowdrops flowering in the glen
And pansies' smiling faces shone
To herald in the spring.

But now a cloud blanks out the sun,
The sky, once blue is dark and grey,
The wind howls down the lane.
Snowflakes floated softly down.
Another and another fell
And faster down they came.

And as the wind in anger blew
The snowflakes danced like fairies' light
And covered all the ground.
'How cold it is,' the flowers said,
And slept again 'neath blanket white.
Frost sparkled all around.

But Winter couldn't keep her hold
Upon the Earth. The sun once more
Sent down her golden rays.
Snow soon in rivers ran away
The flowers shone in bright array
Gone were the winter days.

Snowdrops demure in dresses white
Celandine glowed with golden light
And drifts of crocus grew
The daffodils in yellow shone
As brightly as the midday sun,
Winter's last stand was through.

Barbara Dunning

Courting

We were younger, we first met,
When I first asked her to dance,
When she didn't mind if I was p****d
And I hated dancing;

Spinning, flashing mirror balls,
Old Spice, Hi-Karate and Brut,
From the crimson guys who look like
They have fallen into a tin
Of waste deep white paint.
Doing the splits and pointing their fingers
Like demented traffic cops.
While nauseous patterns race each other across the walls
And the teasing chicks square dance
Around piles of tacky patent leather.
In the bogs the smell of s**tp**svomit'
Sinks full of acrid purple sick,
From the Pernod and Blacks,
Rum and Cokes and cider and Blacks,
Half-digested basket meals marinating,
Garnished with lurid pink lager froth.
French kissing to the last dance smooch,
Like dipping used toilet roll Into an ashtray
Swimming naked in the slop trays.
The tortuous zigzag route home,
Shortening the distance
Up, along, up along, up and along,
Till we reached the vicarage,
Among the long dark shadows of the bone yard,
With its sickly sweet smell of decaying flowers;
In the everlasting peace,
And cold breath of the morning air,
To the secret wall
Where we'd kiss and smoke,
The drizzle teeming down like a giant swarm of midges
Around the head of the lamp post.
We sit and talk.

D Kempthorne

In The Garden

We went into the garden
We went to climb a tree
Up to the little tree house
My daddy made for me.

It has two proper windows,
It also has a door,
And Mummy laid a carpet
Upon its wooden floor.

We also have a table,
And each of us a chair -
Although I haven't mentioned him,
One is for my bear.

I never go without him,
We're happy off the tether
And then up in our tree house
We're safe and snug together.

It's lovely there in summer,
We sit and watch the sky,
And see the fleecy summer clouds
As they go sailing by.

And sometimes in the winter
When we feel very bold,
We go up to our tree house
Although it's very cold.

But we are well-protected,
With hat, coat, scarf so warm.
Mummy makes us put them on
To keep us safe from harm.

Hail or rain or sunshine,
We never have a care,
We're happy in our tree house,
Just me and Teddy Bear.

G Burns

To Dad - Wherever You May Be

Dad, I know you're out there somewhere, a vision so clear
in my mind.
I always look in the crowd for your face, searching for
something familiar.
Would I recognise you if I saw you? Are you close to me or far,
far away?
Do you live just round the corner or have you gone to a distant land?
The last photo I have of you is creased from always being
in my purse.
How many years is it since you saw me, since you hugged me close?
As I grew up you were the hero at the centre of all my stories,
You were the 'if only' to my troubles, the solution to all my problems.

I always told my friends all about you making up what I didn't know.
I rejected the pity that flashed in their eyes; you are my dad,
you are real.
Every year on your birthday, Father's Day and Christmas,
I remembered you.
I always send you a card in the mail labelled Dad with no address.
You never get it I know, but I didn't forget you ever - not once.
Did you forget me?
Am I the heroine in all your stories? Do you imagine what
I'm doing now?
Do you remember what I looked like and search for my face in
the crowd?

Divorce should be about adults who have long since fallen out
of love.
It should never be about taking children from either of their parents.
I have never blamed you Dad, nor did I ever blame Mum.
Laying blame would not have healed over the wounds.
I believe you Dad when you said you'd love me forever,
And I want you to know that I will always love you too.
I hope that one day we'll find each other again
And I hope that it will be one day, very soon.

Zenda Madge

Golden Chairs

She wandered into the empty pavilion
With only the gold cane chairs
Tumbled in a corner;
A half finished jigsaw,
Loosely fitted together -
Symbolic of their love.

Salt air coasted through the open door,
An orchestra strung a sensual tango.
Grouped under fanning palms
The golden chairs were gleaming
In the slant of shoreline sun.

The silken dress of cucumber green,
Cooling her vibrant hair,
She had ended the search.
His hand caressed her neck
Unable to see beyond his shoulders,
She was sand drifting through an hourglass;
A stone fixed between velvet.

A bird of passage with no regrets.
Memory kindled intoxication
A widening of the nostrils,
With unrestricted breath
Shaped by impromptu ease.

Now there was just the voice of waves;
Washing over the gold cane chairs . . .

Veronica Charlwood Ross

Gravity

We spend so much time trying to escape.
Soaring in skyscrapers and aeroplanes,
Hiking up stairways and escalators
Into some wide blue.
We force our feet, fingers, ideas
Like flightless birds grounded by our weight,
And looking oblivion in the eye,
Six billion Icaruses strain to stand
On top of the world.
Cocooned in space suits, silver rockets
Tug us out and onwards
To walk on grey, airless landscapes
To hit a golf ball and instead
Of dropping watch it wait,
Hesitate
A million miles just to see the pause
Between floating and falling.
Flying and dying.
With clipped wings and footprints
Our heavy confession.

Fleur Jones

Old Faith, New Beginnings

You ask too much, except greatness.
Be humble and caring.
Treat your fellow man as
Another human being.

See right from wrong.
Be strong in the faith you chose to belong.
Believe in your ideals, meet others too and
Share your love and friendship.

Remember why you are alive, and accept
Your birth so beautiful and worthwhile.

All this I say to you because knowing the
Knowledge of words to explain how you
Feel is a gift.

Finally, never stop learning, it keeps you young
And when you reach your age of elder years
Look back as those wild oats, grow old and
Look upon your family.
Say, 'I did make it,
But not I. I know my end and know how my end is to be.'

Gillian Robson

A Mother's Lament

My Lord,
was it necessary so to do.
Should not the punishment fit the crime?
But what was my crime? My sin?
Did it demand so ultimate a sacrifice?
My child! My only child!
Conceived in love,
nourished in love.
Born in pain but also in joy.
The perfect flowering of our combined seed
lies now lifeless.
Our life, too, now is dead.
The down of his hair like velvet,
a perfect rosebud shaped his mouth.
His eyes? Ah! His eyes I never saw.
They opened not upon this world.
Was the beauty of our babe such
You deemed it better he should dwell in Heaven?
Was it for this my body was so used?
No, never say that.
Yet I recall Your words.
'I am a jealous God.'
Did You fear love for my Son
would exceed my love for Thee?
Of Your mercy,
Tell me
Lord.

A Baglin

Indian Summer

The dying has begun;
The wrinkling and fading;
The blurring and cooling at breaktime.

Opposite me in the staffroom
A supply teacher, almost me twenty years on
Inhales deeply
And starts on a crossword,
A crossword in a book, almost twenty years old;
A crossword completed in pencil a thousand times
To be rubbed out so carefully,
So gently a thousand times,
To be completed a thousand times more,
If only the paper was not now so thin
For such a sisyphian task.
Fascinated I watch.
He pauses. He inhales deeply,
Slowly looking up with disdain
At my transitory interest,
In someone other than myself.
Coffee drips onto my newly cleaned tie.

The blurring and cooling at breaktime;
The wrinkling and fading;
The dying has begun.

David Morgan

The Dawn

The summer dawn creeps into the house around three am
The summer dawn so silent and pure
The daylight grows silently and purely brighter
As the blackbird tests out his vocal chords
Singularly and softly sweetly and clear
The world is asleep around my habitat
The curtains of the houses are drawn and closed
The garden below seems magically splendid in the silence
A myriad of hues and colour, colour and hues
As the dove and the squirrel search my lawn
For scraps of sustenance
The verdant lawn, green and lush,
Seems sprinkled with heavenly dew
As the silence of the summer dawn strengthens and inspires
Induces calm, pleasance, well being into the soul and heart
The roving sun will rise overhead when it reaches the crest
The world and my neighbours still remaining at rest
The time is four-thirty, this is a summer dawn.

Margaret Bennett

The Big Freeze

I watched as the silver wind blew.
The dazzling sparkle of white teeth,
as snowdrops swiftly fell upon pink tongues.
An array of symbols and patterns on the soft clear cushion
of the earth.
A celebration of arms and hands diving and swaying,
desperate to feel the tickle of a snowflake on a finger.
Excitement bubbled as the girls' grey kilts spun like dizzy
spinning tops,
and the flutter of young voices danced on the slow, ascending air.
I peered below as little crystal angels began to appear in the snow,
their fresh angelic faces smiling and glistening.
Then more classes began to gather in the small circular courtyard,
girls giggling as they slipped on the icy banks
Everyone's faces lit up under that pale morning sky,
opening up their arms,
praising the sender of all those falling luxuries.

Emilie Condie

Whose Life

It's my life she said,
I'll do what I like she said,
                                        and she did.
She didn't listen,
she went her own way,
she experimented with drugs,
she could take what comes she said.
Life was to be lived she said.
For excitement she injected herself with heroin.
The syringe was dirty,
germs invaded her body,
'It's my life,' she said.
But was it!
Now she's dead!

Gladys C'Ailceta

Art Ablaze

When the blaze struck
That warehouse in Leyton
Works of Brit art were lost
By Hirst and Emin
A fifty-million collection
Belonging to Charles Saatchi
What a dreadful shame
That the warehouse was half empty.

Paul Curtis

Losing Brothers

I come wandering in with your milky tea and cornflakes and find you
sitting up in bed, one hand supporting eternity against the
bedroom wall,
I used to be a big girl, five minutes ago, but now I am, just small, and
this much I know with certainty.
In this child, the woman dressed in the soft, white, night-gown,
compared to the old photograph, Scarborough, 1943,
My grandma, newly-wed, sufferingly thin, cannot raise the
dead-weight of the lives gone missing.

My great Uncle George with about four-foot fate bounced off dead -
liked the pap-pap sounds of the motorcars trundling past,
This is a long time ago; Jim, when the gun didn't work, carefully
Collected, recommended dosages of pills in a drawer for weeks,
And then took them all in one go,
And all the hills rush down to the sea here and Gran stands beyond
her limits and of all things imagines in small, neat script,
there was nothing you could do, sealed with a single kiss. It's not
there; it's her anniversary of not really eating.

I remember a day spent walking the stretch from Gran's front steps
To her corner sweet shop, a bottle of bubbly lemon pop going
between us,
He returns it to me later, despairingly, bearing a pint at least of my cup
spill over blood.
The razor upraised, complains of a death of great pleasures;
How many times a day standing behind where you stood but a good
ten years older,
Palms stained as red as he who bought post-pungent cherries at the
market hell,
Much too close to the oozy stage to be handled well.

I find I am not faring better under this late phase of the lighter regime,
The nurses arranging her delicately upon the grey sheets for the
seasonal stay
And my carrying her clumsily from backyard to front,
For months, say, 'Oh dear,' and all of us getting the giggles as we
prise her into the low-slung car,
Her memory slipping down so far and her developing the broad-
brushed feel for detail, perhaps erasing all the bad things I did as a
child; *I* did.

I think of the infinite futility of love, I starve and starve and know no remedy because I know not that I am sick,
See my own reflection in the mirror and take solace that I am ugly and unfit to be touched anymore.
My mind so low I cannot recall the sinister power that silently commanded my ruin,
And thereupon, his sweater tied loose around her waist,
Consolation and heart with the old, dying woman is driven.

Ellen Marsh

On First Publishing

Inside once, not that long ago,
chained by time, silently straining at its leash,
lurked a stifled voice!

Memories nailed down in the recesses
of a scarred mind,
and an aching body - crying out
for the raging torrent of emotions
to cease!

Emotions - buried -
deep, deep, deep
in childhood's grave.
The heart never fully touched,
the mind never fully opened -
closed by fear!

Then a loving compassionate,
Listener of woes,
Touched that heart and mind,
And allowed a little light in!

Flowers cannot grow in the dark,
not for long.
They need light, nurture,
for their seeds to grow, take root,
and reach for the stars!

So happened with my words.
Once long ago, they spoke.
They were silenced through betrayal!

Now those words, separate little entities,
meet and merge,
take the shape of poetry!

Rosie Heartland

Granite Grey

Pulled, ripped taken from
The depths, no gentle caress
Of hand.

Hoisted aloft, transported
Then its fate!

Moulded, chisel, hammer
Created, understated in its
Appearance

Jigsaw, gigantic in proportion
Mechano

Nurtured, a vision yet stark
In its raw natural beauty

Moved, taken hoisted once more
Tall dominant, placed piece
By piece, an end what
Relief

As we at last witness
The cold
Shapes
Of granite grey Aberdeen
Built from the very rock
On which we reside.

Dave Wilkie

The Bubble Of Life

Being with someone that cares for you
Being able to feel the sun on your face
Feel the wind through your hair
Walking through a forest to watch a babbling brook

Seeing the clouds as they race across the sky
At night watching the stars twinkle in the night
Knowing that tomorrow will be here, sure as can be
The thrill as you clinch that deal you have been working on

Thrilling at the thought of being and doing what you want
That excitement as you make love and the pleasure you feel
You laugh just because you can, what the heck it's good to be alive
Receiving that message that makes your heart race

You make of things what you can, enjoying each moment
Being here now is what matters
All things are there for us now and always
The bubble of life for you and for me.

Carole A Cleverdon

The End Of An Era

If bloodthirsty hands can curse the land,
To form an ocean that's made up of tears
The ocean would flood through desert of blood
And each emotion would drown all my fears
If the sun should fall in a big fireball
The sun could then burn away all my woe
Drying the waters that tears have brought us
The sad tears I yearn to no longer flow
If there came a storm to smooth each scorn
Would I surrender to the stormy wind?
Could all these combined cleanse my troubled mind
Cleaning so tender all my past sins
If crushed by the sky we'd no longer cry
No water would shed but first I would pray
To nature's maker, God our creator
The one who had bled for us of today.

Paul McIntyre

A Great Pleasure

I never ever thought it would happen
The way I feel inside, for I feel so great
After all those stupid days I wasted on you
The days I forgot even those unending digits of pi
I don't hate you, for I never hated one
I loved you for hurting me
I loved you for deceiving me
For you taught me a lesson
Never put too much trust in crooks and flirts
Even I won't use that word
She has a motive, money and she makes it
Clear right from the start, but what was yours?
Now you maybe on your search for your next prey
But it won't take long for him to see
You are born the way you are
Are you mad at me?
Are you mad at me because I outsmarted you at your own game
Like man always outsmarted God in His own game?
Did you want to be that same old sentimental fool Shanu?
No, no, no, you get what you richly deserve
You took me for a fool
Thought I would forgive you. *Yes.* I always did
Not anymore, now it's my turn, my girl
I waited and waited and waited
For the right moment when you have no clue at all
When I can turn my tables easily
For I have to crush the viper
Beneath my feet that he can't bite me back
Gratitude is a burden, but revenge is a pleasure
A great pleasure . . .

S Athiparambath

Love

We were the sun in our faces
And ran like wind through corridors of light and air.
We had no ghosts of time to trouble us,
No faltering footsteps or white snow in our hair.

The world was our world, we owned it,
Scattering the careless seeds of youth we danced on rainbows.
Flew over mountains and seas with swift abandon,
Our dreams held no darkness or death, only laughter.

Now as I push your wheelchair on the esplanade,
Avoiding dogs and prams and sandcastled urchins
I look down at my hands, wrinkled like crabs
And marvel that these ancient things belong to me.

And then you turn and look at me and smile
And I forget the lines upon your face
And see you dancing still in the bright of morning
In another time, another air, another place.

Margaret Rose Harris

Roundabout

Going down that road again,
I know I've been here before.
Going round in circles of pain,
but I'm ready for some more.

Travelling through this maze,
this spaghetti junction called life,
trying to find my way
discover my function -
Looking for a slip road
to take me off this trip mode.

Going round in circles down that same old road again,
hazard lights on overdrive - overloading my brain.
Seeing the casualties from the crash sites of my journey through
this life,
reliving the love,
the hate,
the fights.

I'm looking for that turning that leads down that country lane,
seeking a route that will cause the least pain.
But my tyre tracks will betray me
and show the way I went
and reality will follow
and spoil my moment.

William Anthony Ralphson

Consumer

The bread of Heaven is not the bread of life,
It has no material function and it causes no fight, pure like bread
Pushing the darkness to its edge
A symbol of sacrifice not giving into its material ledge,
Even when sunburnt it's whiter than its edge, crispier more
Crunchier, a more tastier pledge,
The sinful butter, the calories, the jam, the marmite, the devil to the
Sacrifice of the lamb,
It's your choice, you choose
Drown in marmite or be saved by the sun.

Paul Blair

Today

Another day,
Arrives today,
Another maybe tomorrow,
To do or be, all that we could,
In each precious one.

To spend with care
While strength there be,
First things in place,
To rest assured,
If God appeared.

No other fear to fear,
He is one being,
To let Him be
In all to do and say,
In all our todays.

Rachel Taylor

Holiday Madness . . .

Arranged for weeks, got to change all the arrangements.
Can I do this, that and the other, please do this now.
Get it done, must go faster, must go at light speed.
Can't do it all in one go.
I will not go if you don't hurry up.
Speed, forget to take the dog for a walk.
Don't turn the gas off, don't switch the lights on timer.
Can't find the stopcock, water will flood everywhere.
Not going to get there, time's getting on, must rush.
Can't find my book, must read on the way.
Pick up the bags, load the car, wish I had a bigger car.
All this stuff but not the kitchen sink as well.
Soon be leaving, got to go. Soon be there . . . I hope.
Kids are screaming, can't go on. There is the site at last.
Unload to find we forgot to pack Granny, no great loss then.
Soak up the sun, hah that's a laugh, nothing but rain.
Two weeks of nothing but wet soggy clothes.
Wet feet and runny noses. Soon be leaving, soon be home.
In sight at last. Why is there smoke, where is my house . . . ?
House burned down by squatters, I am never going
on holiday again!

G Knight

Weeding

Is it selfish?
Our time is valuable.
Hearts full of love,
directed by the head,
embrace each other.
Is it give and take
in equal measure?
Real friends
never ask or demand
too much.
So we weed,
shed and unravel
from constriction.
Tough decisions,
action,
avoids betrayal
of our conscience.
Welcome new growth.

Chris Webb

Goats' Cheese

It is pungent like the odour of a donkey's arse
Or that whiff you might get from dog-soiled grass
So strong in flavour you might just spew
Like with marmite on toast, or a pig's dinner stew.

It's not like solvents that may send you away
Or destroy your life with a cocaine-decay
It's ripping, gritty and boy does it pong
Like a workman's armpits or a prostitute's thong.

Worse than a fart covered in custard
As rich as the burning of hot English mustard
Intense as the fire of a Jamaican chilli-sauce
The taste of the cheese is sharper than, course.

Some eat it with salads, or straight with some wine
Others they cringe, where for them cheddar is fine
Some they plainly choose, just to run far away
Whilst those that sell in markets are lost by the day.

Strange as it seems, there's a cry for this food
It does it for some, as life changes mood
Never understood, as perhaps chocolate ants
The delicacy remains as gross as old sweaty pants.

Don Capo

Who Are You?

Your handwriting profoundly terrifying
The depth of anonymity you assume.
Each time, different styles -
An expressive cursive scrawl
Or straight, narrow and neat.
Each word losing meaning
Questioning my knowledge of you.
Who you are, what you are -
Are you, you?
If the facet you present
Differs each time
Where is the real you?
Are they all you?

Reena Retnam

What Is Life?

Is it a chain of events
Which when one day ends
Never comes back again?

Is life only a dream
Does it only seem
To be what is only an illusion?

Is life a bed of roses
Which sometimes causes
Pain, due to the presence of thorns?

Is life a game
Of losing and regaining fame,
Of bearing with the time, not tame?

What is life?

Is it only a question
That can never be answered;
Cannot be inferred
From the clues, we have?

And is it right
That life is sometimes bright
But sometimes as dark
And scary as an endless night?

All I know is that
I have failed
To solve the puzzle of life.

Perhaps that is what life is
A puzzle, too difficult for me.
So, I ask for the solution -
What is life?

Nivedita Bhattacharjee

My Breeze

Where was the sunshine?
Hidden behind the clouds.
The winds that blew through my life,
did not blow strong enough to push
the clouds away;
I did have a glimpse of the sun,
but it always clouded over again;
Would the dark days ever clear?

Then one day you came into my life,
Gently the sunlight filtered through;
Now as long as I keep near to you,
every day is a summer day,
with clear blue skies,
the clouds have gone . . .

Chris Perrins

Untitled

I have a deeper reason
That only I inscribe
To answer all the questions
That lie behind your eyes
Tide depends upon the moon
The stars rotate eternal
Hours are moments passed too soon
This love revolves continual
For behind your eyes a mirror
Where I see myself defined
And trust myself forever
Into your heart consigned.

Kay Smith

Wedding Day Thoughts

In our joys and sorrows all along the way
The little happenings and doings
Spring up and come to mind
The first time we met
Walked out together in all winds and weather
The attraction, fragrance of being together
Now growing into each other's ways
Wedding day, the first baby, school
Teenager growing up, marriage.
The first grandchild taking the pram for walks
Sit down and natter to other grans and grandads
And in the passing of time the great grandchildren of
lassies and lads
Now we're on our own me and my old Dutch
But they come to visit, bless their loving hearts.
Sometimes the younger ones stay for a holiday.
Sometimes we look out the window and our memories play
Of two people joined together on their wedding day.

George Camp

Conservation

The heron, the lapwing, the snipe and the curlew
Have once again come home,
The skylark too, with them, as the countryside returns
To how it once was,
Following the many years of abuse, it has known.

The hay-meadows - that for years had been missing
Have returned - A 'Golden Brown', to the fields,
'Neath the gaze of the hot summer sun
And the wild flowers, colour and beauty has returned,
To the 'homeland' where their lives had first begun.

Marshlands, reed beds and swamps,
The babbling brooks, rivers and mountain streams,
Now hold within their sparkling waters,
A true reflection of how life once used to be.

The 'clock of time' has moved the fingers forward,
As 'conservation' rings the chimes,
And the hour of 'Mother Nature's' second coming,
(without the need of the asking of forgiveness)
for that which over the years has been destroyed by mankind
has finally arrived.

Bakewell Burt

'I Am The Vine . . .'

When youthful soldier in my prime
Patrolling sun drenched mountain slope,
Amongst some neatly ordered vines,
I passed a man whose weathered hands
Intently tended treasured stocks.
There's some that seemed as gnarled as he
Before inserted grafts restored
Their hope of harvest's gift. It's then
I heard afresh our Lord proclaim
'It's I who am the vine and you
Are called to be a branch designed
To bear the grapes for making wine,
It's you I call to share my cup.'
I also note that shoots that failed
To draw upon the sap of life
Were those that slowly withered, died,
And then were pruned with loving care
For what remained. My youthful cane
Had lain aside for while before
At last I'm firmly fixed and bound
To sturdy stock in place in sun.
Despite for long I'd lagged behind,
It's now I pause to hymn my thanks,
Along with all who've joined these ranks.
In lasting fellowship with all
Who share a common trunk, we find
The strength to bloom and bear our fruits,
By means of constant flow from roots,
Which being hid escapes the mind
Of mate who's yet to hear the call.

Henry Disney

The Slogan

I attended the public rally
To hear the political actors
They came resplendent in their glories
Faces stiff for civic duty.

When the formal chanting started
I fished from behind the echoes
A slogan,
A sweet slogan.

I hugged the slogan with all my heart
Inhaled it into my lungs
Then, sated and tipsy
I tottered towards home.

On my way I met many people
Who had missed the public rally
I showered my borrowed slogan
On my rapt and trusting audience.

I darted here and there
As many scrambled for me
I had become some actor now
Resplendent in my slogan-glory.

Amidst the new pandemonium I saw
A painter by the roadside
He did his strokes oblivious to
That clamour for the slogan-crumbs.

I went to him and he showed me
The cherished labour of his hands
It was that moment of beauty
Which shed some light at last -

I rid myself of triteness
And chose the path of rightness.

Sospeter M Shake

The Feeling At Home

Rove abroad, a faraway country,
experience, suffer, feel many things.
Let me tire, and weary.
Expecting next holiday,
going back home.

In the airport, feel Mum's hug,
on the way, listen kin's regards,
get home, taste family dinner.
Dad cooks personally,
Mum peels the apple,
I, am busy in answering the phone.

Not time difference at all.
Back to Mum's bosom,
fall asleep sweetly until
sunshine besprinkles my body, strongly.
Soya milk, wholewheat bread with fired egg, my favour.
Take a taxi, going to Grandma's place,
they have been waiting for me.
long long time, I can't have the feeling like it.

The feeling at home is hard to say actually,
warm and comfortable, but a little bit sentimental.
After all -
I have to leave home again,
come back here, continue to
experience, suffer, feel . . .

Zhang Wan

Fleeing Fellow

(Time passes like a dream)

We set off in the dark of night.
The ways were a maze
And the journey was long.
The guide was the same
Who had accompanied many
A traveller earlier than me.
Despite escorting generations of men
He still had a fresh and manoeuvring look
Which betrayed no signs of exhaustion.
Pushing and pulling at each other
We continued passing through winding ways.
Intermittently I overtook him,
But most of the time he would lead the way.
Whenever he moved ahead of me,
He said, 'Fellow, I have got a hold on you.'
I just laughed it off,
Supposing his triumph transitory.
On each turn he assumed such a countenance
As if he knew what was to follow.
Unable to resist my innate inquisitiveness,
I asked of him what was going to be.
'Just wait and see,' was his simple answer.
Then suddenly on a turn he vanished,
Leaving a cloud of dust around me.
Perhaps our journey was spread over eons,
But I could imagine nothing than a day's labour.
And the legacy which was left for others
Carried temporary reflections.

Rizwan Saeed Ahmed

Transporter Bridge

Seventy-five metres tall.
Two hundred and ten metres wide.
Suspended is a gondola
That goes from side to side.

Three hundred steps to climb
to almost touch the sky and
from the wooden walkway
imagine tall ships sailing by.

This 'Aerial Ferry' by Arnodin
is almost a century old.
How many people has it carried
What stories could be told?

Above the fast flowing River Usk
the bridge stands out against the sky:
Still giving safe passage to
Newportonians
as it did in days gone by.

Maureen Thomas

Fallen Orchid

In the sluggish, draining, soporific heat
of the Singapore botanic gardens
amongst palm, rubber and banana trees
I escape from the suffocating fumes
of the busy, bustling metropolis,
traffic flowing endlessly as a river.
Some trees have stood over a century,
a raw reminder of our mutability.

We should lock maudlin memories away
but mine cling like leaves on a summer's day.

The exotic birds are like a tropical trance beat,
Yellow butterflies flicker from plant to plant
As I wander past the Swan Lake and Orchard Plaza
Resplendent with fountains and water's soothing sound
And then under the aesthetic arches of golden shower.
There's a rich aroma of orchids: Oncidium,
Yellow Beatrice Ng, Red Renanthera Yen,
Red Ribbon, Tan Mei Ying and many others too.

Here pollution does not defile the air
but how I long to walk without a care.

Cumulus Nimbus clouds threaten the sky,
I hear the menacing tone of thunder
as I feel the silky petals of a fallen orchid
and I inhale its alluring fragrance.
The colours are vibrant: violet and yellow
but an aura of loneliness overwhelms me
as I remember stroking her golden hair
and her own sweet smell knowing we too were doomed.

Soon the orchid will wither as it must,
lose its opulence, turn brown, then to dust.

Guy Fletcher

Heart Of Town

In these grey-blackened streets,
A sound of traffic envelops me.
The soft rush and susurration
Of tyres on wet ground.

I stop for a second outside a chippy,
And watch some girls pass by.
They are laughing and chattering like people
Who know where they are, and are loved.

Moving on to a local pub,
The difference is staggering.
It's impossibly bright and chromed,
Compared to the darkness outside.

I step up to the gleaming bar
Where a jovial barman stands.
I order a pint of my favourite
Ale, in a shining glass.

Looking around the bar for her,
I see my girl in the corner.
And then I'm right where I want to be,
In the centre of town, with her beside me.

David Finlay

Writing On Concrete

Silver sutra
traced nightly by slugs
on a sheet of concrete
outside our door

as beautiful to me
as a Tibetan prayer
in golden ink on
indigo parchment

and as unfathomable

so why did I erase
with one quick sweep
such meticulously laid
down silver leaf?

Jenny Balfour Paul

The Thing That It's About

Think of that lone Bengali
Dancing and dancing, not
For his own delight but for
His God's and he dances, dances
Till he knows he's wholly one
With the Being he's dancing for.

Or those ten dervishes
Whirling and turning as
They whirl on, on up a heavenly
Spiral and finally spin
Right out of themselves leaving
The watchers wonderstruck.

As a portrait painter turns
Willy-nilly as he works
Into the person he's painting
Until he can breathe and relax

As a conductor reaching
The final coda cannot
Separate himself from the music
Straightway to take his bow

And the impassioned poem
Carries its writer with it
To become the two of them jointly
The thing that it's about.

Glencairn Balfour Paul

Brother Earth

I will miss those tubetrack commuters
Tomorrow have faith children and internet users.
A great big onion strides ever bitter,
We are in a big melting pot.
Our odyssey, our beliefs, our souls in compos mentis
How in name of religion, God bless
That Dulcimer live a heartbeat.

Tomorrow the train leaves the station
In hearts from Norfolk to Felixstowe.
That postman in Glasgow, that builder in Rhone,
A vizier in Rotterdam.

A syncopation amongst the rotted and sybaritic
Where is that love as our soldiers die
An elderly ache and children are abused
Who dares to try.
(Vituperation) for decency we say goodbye
And rain salt water from my eye.

Barry Powell

My Humble Abode

Wisteria displays her pale lavender tresses profusely
as she clings proudly to this my humble abode,
watching over a mosaic table
and its silken fluttering visitors
that wait for me to take breakfast.

Smiling daisies like groups of playground children
lead down to gossiping waters,
where the willow in his magnificence
bows protectively, his slender fingers
caressing the land in splendid gesture.

Canadian geese take delight in rendezvousing
in the warmth of the morning sun,
dipping into a mysterious mercury world,
beyond which a buttercup tapestry rises
to blur with an opulent blue canopy.

My humble abode under curious observation
of one small marmalade statue
who now closes his eyes
and begins to purr in quiet satisfaction
and knowledge of this his kingdom.

Elaine Beard

Pot Walloping

This festival takes place
Each and every spring,
Craft stalls sell their wares
Bands perform and sing.

Local people join
With visitors together
Along the sandy beach
No matter what the weather.

To throw the pebbles back
Dislodged by winter gales
Onto the famous ridge
Pot walloping prevails.

Beverly Maiden

Awakening

Intent on love
Searching, longing

Broken by the power of past desires,

Fearful as the abyss of emptiness
Approaches my wounded heart.

Then you appear sweet angel
Arousing my soul from its slumber,

A glance from your dancing eyes
And I am enchanted by beauty

Returning to life
Able to taste love in all its splendour!

J McLaughlin

Alone

Destiny is calling me,
Telling me it's time for me to live my life
That was predestined long ago.
I felt like my life was over
But it had not even begun.
I am a product of this crazy world here
But not truly belonging.
I feel alone even in an overcrowded room.
I need to find somewhere to belong
Before I finally rot inside, die and then fade away
Into nothingness
Still to be alone.

Pam McCormack

A Passion Flower Falls

Inaugurating the word 'Mother'
to a legacy,
From beginning to eternity.

My ma-in-law,
Providing a sense of continuity,
handed down passionately
the most profound gift ever: wisdom.
A pearl glints hidden significantly
trusting its unique rhythm of colours.
Whose value will outlive its appearance.

A mother's expression of love,
nurturing and stimulating,
A marching symphony for the child.
Who, in an oyster shell,
Lay cradled, serenely gathering
the priceless treasure.
Developing layer upon layer
of trailing wisdom
to give life to knowledge.

In my beloved husband she is resonant.
In him, her finest features apparent.
An instinctive inspiration for all.
To inspire she was blessed.
In sky pure points of light assert,
do away with ignorance.
Her legacy re-echoing,
Initiating a new chapter.

Yasmeen Ahmed

Opiate Devil Cake

Pinched soiled fingers sieve white powder
in a hollow bowl of world addiction.
Nations of mixed fruit, cerebrally chopped
and peeled, await blanching of pitted sin.

Sprouting sagacity now in free fall,
is pummelled and beaten into confused mixture
when seeking solace in the sweet narcotic dose
supplied by bitter perennial 'pushers'.

Essential salts of urgency and understanding
are excluded from mixture, enabling materialism
to blend with apathy on large marble slabs.
Now oven ready, mixture will bake in statistics.

The opiate cake is placed in foil of turmoil,
to cook in ignorance during formative years
and provide society with lavish portions
of the sour devilish dish.

Alex Branthwaite

Midnight Joy

I remember last night -
How could I forget your touch.
Electric
as bodies speak -
in words unspoken.

Such a night was this
as time stood still
for our sojourn of love.
Drowning in the dark depths
of our mystical union.

Passion rising
in the molten lava
that is love.

I gave you my heart
last night.
For you to nurture
as one would the early
buds of spring.
Fragile -
Easily broken.

Closer to Heaven -
I have never been.

Nina Graham

Still Life

(22 July 2004)

Curves of maroon slouch astride soft metal tubing.
A bodiless torso drapes on a near-silver back:
Shining loops, slightly-less than half visible
Under the hint of humanity.

Unreadable lettering twists within cloth,
And a contrasting rigidity
Plunges through
And behind
And between,
Yet remains immovable, immutable.

The warmth-giver is cold,
The symbiont parasitical;
Functionless passivity
By the fully-functioning chair it drowns.

Wilson James

Shadows of the 'Purbecks'

The beauty of 'The Purbeck Hills' roam back to ever-charming
'Isle of Purbeck'.
With many joyable sounds to dwell before you.
Array of great shining green beauty undisturbed
Utterly demands respect.

When one stops and ponder away the hours.
In the cool breeze of close to sea
With lovely growth of colourful wild flowers
On the leas.

High above the vastness blue of the sky
And look below in early morning dew dampness
A high-pitched noise of the seagull's cries
On the Purbeck cliff tops
Are a magical sighting
To watch and to stop,
For a while.

Sammy Davis

Togetherness - A Melancholy Tale

'What? I don't need you!'
She said.
Ignoring herself again.
We were Brown bear
And White bear -
Except not bears.
We were Punch
And Judy -
Except not puppets.
We were *right*.
But pride comes
With a fall,
And she fell, alright.
Probably still falling.
But I don't care.
Much.

Jenny Messenger

Another Day!

Just another day,
Watching the world go by.
Just another day,
Listening to her cry.
Moaning;
About her poor little life
Groaning:
About all of her strife,
          Claustrophobic
In her small little mind.
Things pouring out
All of the time
Nobody to trust;
No one but me.
Waiting, forever;
To set herself free.
How do you react
To all of that pain?
What do you say?
How do you explain?
The questions she asks;
You can feel her grief,
'Why did Daddy . . .?'
You can see her disbelief.

Suzanne Lain (19)

Caerphilly Castle

Brooding, silent, here I stand,
As sentinel o'er this lovely land.
Would the brave approach the gate,
To look into my long lost fate.

Hear the ghosts of yesteryear,
And climb my towers, without fear.
Footsteps echo, above, below,
Shadows follow, 'ere you go.

Hear the sound of ghostly battle.
Chain mail, armour, sabres rattle.
Horses hooves, on cobbles clatter,
While tourists look, with eager chatter.

Was this all imagination,
This history of our great nation?
If the stones could only speak.
This is what the tourists seek.

Gwyneth Pritchard

High Street Promenaders

People in the high street walking and mingling.
Large folk and small folk, all seem so busy.
Girls with short jackets, fur collars afloat.
Young boy with crutches, hobbling painfully,
Women in high heeled shoes, strutting uncomfortably.
A man with a high hat pulled down at an angle,
Moving so quickly, his feet lightly tripping.
Striped sweatered daddies, clutching at offspring.

Denim legged ladies with bottoms that wriggle.
Two peak-capped cool kids, drifting and darting
On skateboards that rumble and scrape on the cobbles.
Tired looking mothers with baby bulged buggies.
Fast-food filled hands feeding fat faces.
Roof-high perched pigeons, seeking their supper
With eyes looking down at the crumb-scattered pavements
And the man with the high hat trips by yet again.

Christine Hughes

Pheromone

It's slowly creepin'
But it's narrow
And I know
It's a love not meant for me
No time to breathe in
It keeps flowing
It's growing
Heavier than gravity
I thought I destroyed this emotion
Such a wonder I ever discovered you
But I've got nothing to make you see me
Should be so simple but I don't know how to
When my everything builds to perfect
It must be time for it all to come crashing down
A single word could crush my existence
But it all depends on how you want me around
Here it comes again
A revision
A vision
A dream that whispers to me
No time to breathe in
It keeps flowing
It's growing
Heavier than gravity
I look through myself to see inside
But I must go beyond to see into you
Seemed so perfect yet still infinite
Just afraid I'll find answers to the obtuse
And if I never see your face again
Please understand that there was nothing I could do
Because I don't want to have to be this
When all I ever wanted was to be with you

Steve Morris

A Lullaby To The Child I Will One Day Have

Go to sleep,
go to sleep little angel,
my little angel
in the heavens above.
Shut your eyes
and dream of a mother's embrace
in the years to come.
Listen to the music of her voice
and play with her hanging hair
as she bends down,
as she reaches out to you,
to hold you.
Let her take the cares away
let her sing you to sleep . . .
Go to sleep,
go to sleep my baby
and wake up inside me.

AnnaMaria Zammit

Fool Or Wise

If every boy and girl
every man and woman
in this world
said no to fighting
what then . . . ?

If every boy and girl
every man and woman
in this world
rejected to touch weapons
what then . . . ?

If every boy and girl
every man and woman
in this world
became conscious
about their actions
what then . . . ?

If every boy and girl
every man and woman
in this world
became conscious
about using love
what then . . . ?

Am I a fool or
am I wise?

Genio Engen

The Night Bus To Philly

A Brit lady just arrived in Yankie Stadie country,
Landed on a night bus to Philly
In the pitch-dark. Someone sat on the back seat
Of the driver. No one else drove in the dark, yet
Someone in the dark became sinister - oh well,
Remembered incidents in California bus-wise,
Alone, with a man beside my pocket.

'Mind your purse,' a woman warned.

Really, there was nothing there but . . . in the dark

All backs are fronts, all hands hold guns or knives,
All faces wear a mask.

In the dark, you can guess no man's context,
Only the immediate feel
So you know it's not a woman but a man.
Before the dark, you stole a glance at his shape,
Like the cleaner colour of a cat at finding light
Before the night paints him black
And ready for hunting.

On arrival there, the night swallows us whole,
And the sleazy thirteenth street welcomes us into
Its weary embrace.
Tellies on at armchairs as we wait
To be delivered, a lot of pockets in a queue
Of blue movies.

Diane Burrow

A Time

It was a time when a child was expected to be a child.
Leaving the more difficult things for one
More equipped to handle them.
It was time when things where easier,
And your soulmate became your partner for life.
It was a time when things were different.

Ise Obomhense

The Fourth Age

There is another time these days,
Youth, prime and age are not the sum:
Follows the age of incapacity,
Meaning dependence on the care of others -
Other mere strangers -
When mind and body fail and independence
Turns to a dream, vanishing like smoke on a gusty day.

I blame the doctors for this cruel state,
The naïve life preservers who insist
On forcing forward the unending days,
Ignoring dignity or grace,
Or proper time.

We have the right to choose our closing moment:
We should not lave such grave decisions to a callow youth,
Nurtured on thoughtless optimism,
Fresh from life-adoring school,
Who has no concept of the merciful coup dé grace
And thinks that living death is life.

Sylvia Dewhirst

Set Me Free

I wanna feel the sand in between my toes
Only the ocean knows how good it feels.

I wanna swim out far where no one can see me
Except the fish, they bite my toes,
I love it, it tickles.

I wanna lay in the grass where no one can see me
But the butterflies,
The beautiful butterflies.

I wanna sing out loud where no one can hear me
But the birds, I love them, they accept me.

Set me free now, set me free
Let me be now, let me be
Let me be now who I wanna be
Let me be now, let me be.

I wanna run in the rain
And come home to you soaking wet.

Only nature can keep me in touch with my soul
Only nature can make me feel so wonderful
Only nature can make me feel in touch with God
Only nature can help me to find true love I feel with you.

Sima Fisher

Judgement

If I lay bare my soul
Will you treat me gently
Accept my strengths and weakness
And judge me not?

If I open up my heart
Will you see the love, the pain
Accept my fears, my passion
And judge me not.

If I share my mind
Will you listen to all my hopes, my plans
Accept my dreams
And judge me not?

If I show you the real me
Will you want to stay
Accept me for all that I am
And judge me not?

Suzanne Thorne

Jessica

Jessica:
Replica of Clive,
I've always found,
Round the mouth and eyes;
Surprise to see the girlishness,
This pretty mop so fair:
Hair of downy corn;
Fawn in early sturdy toddle.
Waddle off you little dolly.
Jolly soon your world unfolds,
Holds you rapt in play:
Clay to daub and taste;
Faced with myriad toys:
Joys of each simple thing
Bring your crinkled smile,
While the blue, blue gaze flatters -
(Matters not what you say).
Gay and cute as ever,
Never spoiled and petulant,
Bent on wilful blare -
Where I cannot but praise:
Days serene and secure;
Pure parental love.
Above all else, a welded pair
Share Jessica.

Eileen Ellis-Whitfield

The Tree Of Life

(Dedicated to my children)

I am the tree of your life,
And you my children are its four sturdy branches,
My grandchildren are the buds reaching out,
For light, air, nutrients to make them grow,
Your wings are not big enough to go round me,
To hug me in times of trouble and sadness,
But fear not, my four beautiful babies,
For I know you are there strong and true,
As we are far apart so we are united,
United in our love and harmony for each other,
As I pray for you all my little ones,
I beg for forgiveness in any misdeeds,
That I may have landed on your plate,
But please remember the wings of your life,
Are small in comparison to my large tree,
And I don't mind if you cannot reach me,
Because you are there my precious four,
Sturdy strong branches growing thriving honest and true,
Feed your buds well my children,
As it is only you that can,
Make them strong with your rearing and love,
So you, can then become the tree of life,
When my tiredness and loss of sap has made me no more,
And so continues the cycle forever,
Never ceasing to amaze man,
My precious loves,
Please do all that you can.

Kathryn Evans

Daughter Of Zion

Among all flowers the rose is the most beautiful,
How right they are to adore you.
Dark, yet lovely, oh daughter of Zion,
Dark like the tents of Kedar.
Like the tent of Solomon, the perfect beauty.
Tell me you whom I love, where you gaze your flock
And where you rest your sheep at midday?
I liken you to a mare
Harnessed to one of the chariots of Pharaoh the king.
Your cheeks are beautiful with earrings,
Your neck with strings of jewels.
How beautiful you are, oh how beautiful.
Like a lily among thorns is my darling among the maidens,
Like an apple tree among the trees of the forest is my love.
I delight to sit in her shade and her fruit is sweet to my taste.
Strengthen me with raisins, refresh me with apples,
For I am faint with love.
Her left arm is under my head and right arm embraces me.
Listen my love, listen to me,
Never have I looked upon anything as beautiful as you.
You are someone dear to my heart so beautiful.
You are surrounded by beauty, love and in trick;
You are chosen to be mine.
The greatest mystery of life is who we truly love.
How beautiful you are .
The excellence of beauty
I love you always, no matter the distance
I can't afford to miss you.
The beauty of creation.

Ifeanyi Osuoha

Free

Even through the night
The fight still goes on
To survive in this life
To revive those thrills
Of ever learning more skills
Feeding my yearning to be free,
To flee from all aggression
As though it were depression
To free my mind and senses
And release myself from strain and tenseness.

My spirit flows in endless time,
But never do I mind
Knowing freedom is mine.

Debra Ayis

All Alone

(Dedicated to my son Jordan, sorry we left you alone)

All alone with his thoughts, no parents for comfort
Not knowing the future, or what it would bring
Brother so sick, Mum and Dad staying with him
They know the score, why must he stay behind?

All alone felt forgotten, feeling sad and so rotten
Worried and scared, would life be the same?
So ill was his brother, the last time he saw him
Burned in his mind, forever to stay.

All alone to continue, his normal routine
In a world of despair, who could keep themselves keen
Try hard to put fear, from out of his mind
But people keep asking, trying hard to be kind.

All alone he would travel, to the hospital and back
Holding in tears, trying hard not to crack
Then alone in his bedroom, the house quiet and empty
Came the fears and the tears, and the nightmares a plenty.

Now home are his parents, and so is his brother
Life back as it was, no I doubt it will ever
Where is he now, out having fun with his mates?
No, all alone in his bedroom, he just sits and waits.

David Ironmonger

Papa

I see your shadow patrolling the house
I see your eyes glaring at me
With anger and disgust
I see your lips move
Hurling insults and abuse
I see your anger stirring
Waiting to thrust.

It strikes me hard, I am taken aback
Years of this, I should have been numb.
But how do you get used to it?
How do you stop?
A strike that goes straight to one's heart

Papa, did you ever love me through my years?
Did I embody all of your fears?

When on my wedding day, you gave me away.
I looked at you for a moment.
Then, a tear fell at the corner of your eye,
To my new husband you said,
'I give you my child, care for her.
Care for her better than I have . . . '

Nancy Lim

Immobilize

Emotion surfacing
A long forgotten sensation
I didn't ask for it
The good, the bad, pushed aside
At the second I heard your voice
I don't know how to feel anymore
I'm sure you'll show me the way
Break my rigid shield
Defrost my frozen soul
And with winter closing in
It'd be nice to have the warmth
That only you can give
But with that warmth
Comes something I despise
A weakness in myself
A hole in my heart
But you don't know me anymore
And you don't care about me either
I know your secret intentions
Just to spite me, you lead me on
Your alter ego can shatter me later.

Crystal Langford

Why?

I cannot find my words
In the real world,
I cannot find a way in the real world,
It is just a waiting of nowhere and nothing,
I collapse to my knees and pray,
I pray of finding reasons to exist,
I pray of listening in quiet
A scary welcome of a life
I never ask to have,
And still I'm waiting for an answer,
Why?

Cristina Evis

Fighting The Lost Battle

I don't want you to stand next to me
Telling me it'll be all right,
And I don't want you holding my hand
I don't need those kind of lies.
For what we had is over now
There can be no turning back
So please will you just walk away
Don't stand here on impact.
Time refused to wait for you and I
It just couldn't bear to see,
Watching us stand alone in silence
Time gave up on you and me.
Oh, nobody here is to blame
Only the truth can understand
And yesterday holds all secrets
The answers aren't here in our hands.
So do not waste any more time
On wondering where we went wrong,
You're only fighting a battle
But the battle just cannot be won.
I'm sure I'll always love you, forever
I do not doubt what I stand here and feel,
But I know that we cannot stay entwined
So I'll leave these emotions securely concealed.
So please give up all weapons and tears
Surrender before we come undone
Just stop trying to win the battle
For this battle can never be won.

J Hope-Kirk

You Never Told Me

You showed me how to love again,
With passion that made me speechless.
Two fiery arms to embrace my feelings,
Greeted me with loving care.
You taught me a different language,
With words not to be spoken but felt.
You allowed my feelings to flow,
Like an infinite stream of happiness.
It was you my dear who taught me,
To see beyond the borderlines.
The lines I was so scared to cross,
You held my hand and helped me over.
It was on this side I saw rainbows,
And walked by your side.
You showed me it was okay to be afraid,
For you would be my comfort.
But you never showed me how to live without you,
Or told me my stream would run dry.
I was never told my fiery arms would turn icy,
Like hypothermic hands clasping my heart.
You never taught me that dreams turned to nightmares,
Making sleep impossible.
So I cross back over borderlines,
On my own this time.
I see rainbows no more.

Nicola Jayne Turner

So Brief

No one speaks and no one coughs
Everyone waits the silence to last.
The curtains drawn, the lights cut out.
The patients strain to hear the news,
A friend they've known, but oh so brief,
But now entombed in a family's grief.

John Hiron

Here We Are Again

And here we are again
My heart is barren,
Lost amongst a sea of tears.
Weeping for a love that's lost
A hope that's lost,
A fear now creeping ever onward
Towards a resolution
Which I pray will never come.
I feel the truth crawl within my soul,
I know it,
I feel it,
Trapped beneath rose-tinted denial.
Where have the days gone?
And where will they lead us
Together or alone?
I fear my own darkness,
To travel alone without you,
As it would be to lose a piece of my soul
- The purest piece.

Victoria Stothard

Prism

Without desire
And without hope
A sharp cornered piece of glass
Am I.
A guideless beam of pure light
Touched my body
And I played with
Seven colours.
The lovers of fun
Gathered around me
To witness the show
It was not
A manifestation of myself
It was a miracle
Of pure light.
None of the seven colours
Were mine.

Amit Gupta

System Of Madness

I once wore a madman's clothes
But now am meek and mild.

The wildness of a mute child
Made my heart sing.

The sadness of the spring
Sprang death from the slain birds sailing.

Today, I walk in the white giant's thigh.
I cry for the moon but the moon is chalk.

I once wore a madman's clothes
But now am meek and mild.

You're getting young, you're getting young,
Youth tastes in the mouth.
All rot is sucked away by words.

I sing for the slain birds sailing.
Clocks tick. This Earth is steadied.

Faith. Faith firmly fixed. Faith
Decries or else no faith.

Once I wore a madman's clothes
But now am meek and mild.

This child is full of graves.

We were all catalysts but now
After - well after the big bang -
A lot of us are pissed!

James Bellamy

Apollo's Songs

It was the night I met Apollo's songs,
They came to me in a long and vivid dream,
A spiral of waves,
Descending upon my soul,
And I knew then it had to happen.

It came to me on a quiet dusky night,
And sped through my flesh like a warm wind,
Dancing on my skin,
Sucking the roots,
A new beginning was about to begin.

It put reality in a small box,
And laughed and the moon smiled,
The stars were singing,
And my head was ringing with new visions,
Scores of angels danced upon my senses,
Bringing the new visions
Laced with deep haven and outer broken barriers.

You can't involve yourself with miscellaneous practices,
When there awaits foundries of other words to acclaim,
I want to acquaint these worlds,
I want to touch, feel and taste them,
For they do beckon me,
The deep dark worlds of the unknown,
Inside distant dimensions,
From which there is no escape,
An infinite duel,
Sunk beneath a lonely lake.

Paul Mackenzie

Boundary

I've found my boundary in you
I looked into the distance and there you were
I turned to the past and met your gaze
I've yearned for this and faithful time produced.
I no longer have to choose.
When I look into the future,
My peace is filled.
So, no more backward glances at yesterday,
My hopes are realised.
I've found my boundary in you.

Tula Benson

Sparks Of Life

(Thoughts on a recently deceased relative)

In the darkness a small spark appears,
This spark of life is still there.
From spark to flame and to light,
To sunshine with powerful life.

There is a new beginning,
Dividing, splitting
Multiplying, replacing,
Multiplying and increasing
But also dying.

For what end?
Will it last?
What will the future be,
And will it last?

New creations,
New beginning,
And new life,
Then another ending.
Is that eternity?

All is quiet,
Full of thoughts,
Planning and full of hope,
But is this an end?

Stillness swallows him
No more desire,
No more hope,
Life has gone forever.

But new life carries on.
Love and expectations
And hopes for his *children.*

Milly Saunders Farren

Schoolcide

In my schooldays I had a really hard time, the others were cruel,
nasty and mean,
They tortured my days and I still have horrible dreams about it at night,
They bit me and hit me and threw chalk at me in class,
They smacked me with rulers and put my desk out in the hall.

I was called names like stupid and slow,
There was no end to the ridicule I faced every day,
When that didn't work they drugged me and tried to have me expelled,
It wasn't my fault that I couldn't do times tables or spell . . .

Bullies and thugs are things that I could deal with,
But this was the teachers and they made my schooldays hell
Now I may be backward, I may even be slow
But there is one thing that even I know

Why the schoolcide rate was so high in the sixties!
School was no fun for me as I am dyslexic and have ADHD beside.

Just ian

Dreams

I was waiting for the great holy saadu today.
Saadu, worshipper of God graced the land of mine.
I waited as I looked at the eight eggs in my basket.
Has one cracked? No, it's me; my mind is playing tricks again.
He enters my home gracing with greatness,
I offered him some food.
'Ask me,' he says to me, 'what do you want to say?'
'Please saadu; tell me which of my eight eggs will crack?'
The saadu replies, 'Do you really want to know?'
'Yes I do,' I say joyfully 'please get this burden off my mind.'
'I can't see any egg cracking,' the saadu replies
'not one will crack.'
I turned around for a second then turned back to ask why this was
Going to happen to me, but the saadu had vanished
from the air he came.

Rajesh Sharma

Untitled

The birds that sang in the springtime, and all the summer long
The blackbird and robin that thrilled my heart
With their happy trilling songs are silent now.
The laugher and voices of children that float on the summer air
The greetings of folks as they pass the gate,
'Good morning, nice day' or 'Hello.' *They are silent now.*
The crackle of leaves in the woodland
Or raindrops come pattering down
Majestic thunder that shakes the sky, the falling of chestnuts, summer has flown. *All is silent now.*
The tinkle of cups on their saucers, the kettle that whistles for tea.
The voice of my friend who calls, 'I'm home'
The sounds which meant so much to me are silent now.
The sound of the lovely church organ, the pastor leading in prayer.
The gentle rustling of hymn book leaves
As we find words of comfort and cheer *All is silent now.*
The beauty of Handel's messiah, the aria, the chorus, the whole.
Divine words and glorious music
That hold both the mind and the soul. *There is silence now.*
So my friends value your hearing, it's a gift so precious and rare.
You will find once it's gone, life is never the same
As when you can say, *'I can hear.'*

Elsie Barker

If Only

If only - life was like it used to be,
No more mugging or knives to see.
Elderly people who have survived the wars
Are afraid, and many live behind locked doors.

If only - the world was a better place
Where people think before they rob and take.
Some blame unemployment, some the families -
It's an unfair society where people fear calamities.

If only - the young had lived years ago
When people helped each other and were prepared to do so.
Life was hard but most people were happy,
There were good neighbours and people were chatty.

If only - loneliness was a thing of the past,
Where people would smile at each other and make it last.
Friendships made and our lives would improve,
There would be something to live for and brighten their mood.

If only - greed and possessions were not thought of so much
And people were satisfied and enjoyed people's trust.
Let's hope in the next century our lives will be safe
And God above will stop the suffering and hate.

B Metcalfe

Organiser Bags

Organiser bags
Are not uncommon wares,
I had one as a sister
For very many years.

If someone had a problem
She'd zip him in a pouch,
He'd not escape as easily
From there as from a couch!

She'd put the world to rights each day,
As well as every night.
So, if someone took full note of her
It damn well serves them right!

George A Tanner

The Residential Home

Silent they sit on the chair in the home
Kitty, Mabel and Kath
Adelane goes to the room to watch tele
Jessie has just had a bath.
Elizabeth always looks after Ivy
In a motherly way
While Vera is always singing
To make it a happy day.
Mabel gets cross when left on a chair
She shouts at the carers and says they don't care
Kath says her dinner is mashed up too much
Thank God the carers have that tender touch.
Kitty is kind and friends with Mabel
And helps her when she misbehaves at the table
When Vera keeps asking for food all the time
Adelane moans and starts to whine.
She's tutting and moaning over any little noise
While Jessie is patient and has so much poise.
Ivy is quite a lovely lady, first up the table asking for gravy.
The carers are wonderful and do their best
I'm sure they'll be glad to have a rest.
I take my keyboard, they all have a sing
To see them happy is a wonderful thing.

Corale Andrews

The Bruise

I didn't notice it at first
I felt the hurt, the pain was worst
But after you had knocked me there
And then had gone, it began to appear.

Poppy red at first as I slowly bled
Then purple as my anger spread
Then with yellow as I began to fear
And then black as my mood became clear.

But you never noticed my bandage
Perhaps I had covered most of the damage
And it was you who felt you have been used
And not me at all, so badly bruised.

Paul Wright

Iraqi Folly

Constantly we hear their cries
From a sad and ravaged land
When warplanes with lethal skill
Deal death daily, from the skies
With armies that seize terrain
To liberate, they say;
The people from the despotic regime
Of their ruler, Saddam Hussain
In conscience it does not equate
That freedom is the goal
Or to save the world from WMD
As minds more devious are at work
The reasons will negate
When all is done, the war is won
What then shall be the call
Peace or insurrection?
I fear the aftermath for all.

William F Park

Sycamore Seeds

I still see them
Furled tightly together,
Two young sycamore seeds
Preparing to fly.
I feel them
Fluttering,
Twirling and somersaulting,
As free as if I were made of air.
I still cradle them,
Hand across my belly
Clutching my empty womb.
The seeds of sycamore
Whirl together about me,
Flying free.

Sarah Howard

As A Cloud

My life's journey is almost complete and I
reflect upon the events I have encountered.

No one escapes times of sadness and pain but hopefully,
happier occasions have helped us face life setbacks.

I remember with great fondness, so many people.
Those I have loved deeply, are no longer here,
yet, I feel them near me.

Though clouds may vanish from sight,
they do not die, they appear in another place,
Soon, I shall be somewhere else,
In a place where pain and suffering are banished.

Like a stream, I shall flow to a heavenly ocean,
my spirit clothed in immortality.
This is Christ's promise and this is my faith.

J Thomas

Turning A Blind Eye

We lay stifled by the silence,
Smothering us both like a blanket,
Wrapping ourselves in each other's unease.
Stale, sticky air hung between us -
Set with the words that weren't said.

Hair sprawled over your face like seaweed -
Bed slept and tangled like the sheets
A dark thicket through which you were peering,
Like a child playing hide-and-seek.
You wished the hunter wouldn't find you.

Then you chanced meeting my eye
And filled the gap between us -
Your sweet breath on the tip of my tongue -
Temporarily chasing my demons
Though you knew I saw the lie.

C Bareham

River Terrig

For the most part, a lazy ambling brook
Chattering over the bleached stones,
Meandering through rough boulders
Strewn untidily in its leisurely path.
Cows and sheep quench their thirst,
Churning up silt, muddying the water.
The riverbank, home to small mammals
Scurrying to and fro among the weeds.
Heavy rain transforms the stream's torpor
Into an angry torrent, frothing and raging,
The turbulence carries all before it.
The precipitation ceases, the turmoil subsides.
The rampaging and bubbling fury spent,
The water slows to a dilatory trickle.
The River Terrig continues on its course.

Rose-Mary Gower

Were You There?

Were you there, were you there, in Trafalgar Square
With the crowds all rejoicing in Trafalgar square?
By Eros and fountain, this was where
2012 was ours with laughter, no frown
In London Town, in London Town.

Were you there, were you there, in Tavistock Square,
When they blew up a bus in Tavistock Square?
And killed all those folk, they hadn't a prayer.
The dead and the dying lay all around
In London Town, in London Town.

Were you there, were you there, in Russell Square
King's Cross too, near Russell Square?
They blew them up, they didn't care,
As they shattered the tubes in the underground,
In London Town, in London Town.

Were you there, were you there, in old Sloane Square
With all the Rangers in old Sloane Square?
Coronation passed by with pomp and flair
And royalty came with sovereign crown,
In London Town, in London Town.

Were you there, were you there, in Parliament Square
On that fateful day in Parliament Square?
Guy Fawkes was foiled by a policeman's stare
His fireworks failed, his plot confound,
In London Town, in London Town.

Were you there, were you there, in Eaton square,
Or perhaps instead in rich Mayfair?
Both hosted the plague and doodlebug fare
Of those that survived, not one fell down
In London Town, in London Town.

Let all her enemies take heed and beware
Our pride and spirit, you will never outwear.
And yes, indeed, we *all* were there
There's no finer city, we proudly profound
Than dear old London, *old* London Town.

Maurice Bailey

Untitled

Life in these corridors is never dull.
Each one with his/her mission to unfold,
Staggers through these corridors day in, day out
Learning, studying, teaching, caring, serving or seeking
In the corridors of life we meet fellow travellers
Who touch and enrich or begins in big or tiny drops
This touch may not inspire recognition inspirit
As we all take to different directions
Mindful of our own missions
But the touch remains and finds a place within the soul
Seasons of life may come and go
But the touch stays forever connected.

Meg Aku Sika

In This Life

In the east the morning sun
Red ambers in the sky
Peeping o're the great North Sea
A familiar sight for me.

The Cornish coast
A different sight
When evening comes along
Cliffs change to glowing hues
Where seagulls belong.

I've sat for hours
On Great Orme rocks
To watch the sun go down
Until the darkness blocks
The busy, bustling town.

I've sailed the Channel, ferrywise
And tossed in the Bay of Biscay
Never seen the raging sea
So frothy, white and misty.

In Norway a mountain lies
To block the sun rays out
Solid granite crystal air
God's world have no doubt.

Pauline Burton

Good Heavens

News of the world
I'm in bed with an angel
Smoky candlelight shimmering
Gently on his skin
Wings folded, gorgeous from every angle
Can't take my eyes off him
Magnet beers on the carpet
I'll have less tonic, more gin
As soon as he kicked his steel-capped boots off
There wasn't time to be coy or prim
Smile soft his eyes mirror bright
Scoop me up and hold me tight
I've been good 'til I'm sick of it
Trying to do what's right
How can something this good be a sin?
It's sudden joy
It's hell being an angel
You always have to be bright
We will touch Heaven by morning
So, go on, darling
Be a devil tonight.

Sue Woodbine

Turmoil

How light the light, birds in flight
Sheltering in a vibrant sky
Clinging with obstinacy above the raging seas
A moon in frenzy
Remote winds groan.
Anguish perilously leads the lost
They go downwards to a subterranean obscurity.
The breezes then turn tranquil
They hold their heads with shame.
And bring forth a perpetual flame
To drift forth, towards port
Far beyond the horizon.
Onward to an enduring peace.

Elaine Priscilla Kilshaw

To Those Who Believe

Tonight we are told a wondrous sight we will behold,
It's the eve of the second coming,
So much excitement, the audience humming,
For months now great expectancy in the air,
After much secrecy, the moment we've waited for is here.
The audience is asked to clap and cheer,
We have been sent one from above, full of compassion,
One who really does care, and from this day forth,
He is to be known as the lord and master Tony Blair.

Could it be with motives quite sinister,
To ensure a third term as Prime Minister?
All your sins are to be washed away,
But there's a price to pay.
Dear voters gather round, help me rid the world,
Of the evil one, known as the pound.
It has to go to make way for the Euro.
So from today, as you will see, I shall decree,
The pound will no longer be around.

Then I can claim in my name, my rightful title,
Of Lord of Europe, leaving you no hope.
This will pass without a hitch,
As he orders us the pound to ditch.
And right across Europe, we're told,
The euro you will use,
Because like it or not, it's all you've got,
And after all it's only money,
Praise be to the lord and master Tony.

David Parker

A Winter's Symphony

Purple and grey winter skies,
Bitterly cold air, night is drawing in,
The land doesn't appear to have a single care.

Snow-covered fields stretch for miles,
The bare eerie trees casting no shadows
As the snow lies on their branches in perfect little piles.

Silence fills the air, the light slowly fades,
A fox moves quickly through the snow
Searching for food to get him through the cold winter days.

Nothing for miles not even a road,
Nature is the master,
The snow-filled sky dominates the horizon heavy and low
As if straining under its impending load.

Everything is silent, nothing makes a sound,
Winter has arrived,
The Derbyshire hills it has found.

Wendy Coulson

London 7/7

Yesterday London wins to host the Olympics 2012
And this vibrant city is jubilant in cheers
But today it has halted to a bombing spree
And this shaken city is now flowing in tears.

Chaotic destruction caused by cowards determined by war
Explosions rip apart a crowded bus and the busy underground
Commuters are the innocent victims in these barbaric attacks
Trapped by harrowing screams to a blasting sound.

The trauma is etched on shell-shocked faces
As reports appear on news bulletins worldwide
Heartache is felt for the loved ones injured and missing
Grievance sets in for the many who have died.

It's not clear who's credited for these attacks
If credit is the word that one would use
But this rocked city is adamant it will move on
Promising this is a battle they will not lose.

Mairtin Kelly

Togetherness

Lazy afternoons were spent idly and wily. As
Seen by 'brothers' from opposite sides of the fence,
Brought together by fate.
    Now in positive repose, opposed in
Friendly banality, tranquil in tranquilization.
A hospital ward for the afflicted. Couldn't decry
The need for support, self help was each others
Shoulder to lean on and cry on.
    Talking animatedly over a game of
Chess. Which was necessary to take up
The time which ensued to endless boredom.
    A kingdom of depression not keen to
Be partook of. A feast for the over taxed
Short-sighted and blighted.
    Now in passive bliss
Whiling away the continuity of the dull
Life in a locked ward. Endlessly waiting
For the evenings-awakening to bring about
Sleep richly deserved.
    Quietly, contemplative smoking
Heavily to wile away the fatigue brought
To bear on shoulders gaunt with worry, burn
Out of all frustrated ambiguities.
    Afflicted to the last staunch,
So it seems. A paradox of afflictions. One
Needed to have rotgut not to notice.
    A strong stomach would suffice -
All the influence, didn't even seem seemly taken on
Board, the foulest of tobacco smells and body
Aromas. Though to end it all the spirits, they
Would eventually be so together. That's what being one
Is all about.

Curven Marshall-Howell

The End Of The Affair

How we yearned to be with each other,
Those first few months of meeting,
The sun shone so it seemed all the time,
And life was good my sweetling.

Then as we learned each other's funny ways,
Things began to sour,
The sunshine was lost and the clouds moved in,
And oh how lonely the midnight hour.

We stumbled on trying again,
To bring back the laugher and glow,
But time came all too soon,
And we knew one had to go.

Suddenly there was sadness and pain,
Once again the *we* became *I,*
Alone with memories of happiness,
Always ending with a long, long sigh.

'Parting is such sweet sorrow,' so the poet wrote,
The having of life itself felt dead,
Goodbye is never easy; in fact it's very hard,
However everything comes to an end and all has been said.

Sheila Hodgkins

I Won't Be A Minute

'I won't be a minute,'
Or so the nurse said.
That minute's like hours,
When you're ill in bed.

You press your help button,
And the words that you hear.
'I will be back in a minute,
To help you my dear.'

Now your laxative's working,
You're in a real stew.
You press your help button,
Oh what can you do!

Your nurse arrives,
Alas, it's too late
She should have answered your help button
And not tempted fate!

M Smale

Street Lad

The little lad had been knocked down
By a lorry in the night,
He'd been sleeping rough out in the town
And had gone to find a bite,
He was lonely, cold and hungry
Ran across the busy road
The driver didn't see him there
As he drove on with his load.

The ambulance came and took him
To the hospital close by,
The little lad was badly hurt
They feared that he might die.
They tended him with loving care
And watched him day by day
But he grew weaker as they watched
All they could do was pray.

At last he opened up his eyes
'Am I in Heaven,' he said
'And is that God all dressed in white
Standing by my bed?'
A smile then formed upon his lips,
His face seemed filled with light.
The doctor could not hold his tears
As the laddie lost his fight.

Mary Stoner

How To Write Poetry And Lose Friends

I had friends before I wrote poetry
Now, I have none.
The muse lured me away from them.
Under her spell I
Wrote like a demon loose from Hell.
I secluded myself.
Sipped absinthe,
Scribbled by candlelight,
Sweated blood and never slept.
My friends thought I was unwell,
My behaviour strange.
They stopped visiting as
I ignored their calls,
Refused their invites for tea and cake.
By night I was driven like a fiend possessed.
Writing and writing, dipping my pen in absinthe,
My mind in dreams,
Finally emerging to recite my poems
Only to find I had no friends.

I had friends before I wrote poetry
Now, I have none.
They have all gone
And all I have are my poems.

Roman Suchyj

Beyond The Veil

I am nothing.
One small particle of the human race,
Held in wonder by what has been,
Awed by the great eternal space
And mysteries yet unseen.
Just a veil divides us transparent . . . thin,
Hiding the wonders of tomorrow
And the next complex thing,
Bringing us joy or sorrow.
Will it be the prize for which we dream?
Evolving endless, countless changes
Into the new world for which men scheme,
I know not the enormity of what it ranges
For I am nothing.

Dorothy Walker

Wake Up, O Man!

Wake up, o Man, 'ere it's too late,
Redeem your reputation;
What God ordained, you all must heed,
Or reap His retribution.

To head your household, it is said,
Quite clearly it is written;
Your womenfolk and offspring too,
Must do as you have bidden.

A partnership, a marriage blessed,
Respect received and shown
Responsibility then falls
On women folk to own.

Not to put down or to malign,
But a partnership upheld,
Encouragement and two-way love,
Marriage vows then set to weld.

Offspring too will learn future roles,
As male and female parents,
A father as a role model,
And mother always present.

Behind a fulfilled man, it's said,
A dutiful wife is found;
The roles ordained by God then must
With contented peace abound.

Janet Bowen

The Final Goodbye

I am gathered here at your final departure
You lived you life so humbly almost a martyr
A friend so loyal, a friend so true
That I had always in you
You were always there for me come rain or shine
We'd walk and talk with your hand held in mine
Those days I will miss, they are no more
But I will wait till I am again at your side once more.

Patricia A Taylor

Day One World, The Night Another

Up and out too long on a torn wild sky
Not in rising or in hanging, but dozing
Forgetting its weightlessness
The bleary sun's bloodshot red ring
Drops sinking down behind
The blackened, knuckled rump of hill
As dark looms over a booming bay.

The lifting sea salt scowling wind, coarse as sand
Blast, lashing cliff and buffing stone; shifting inland
Bent on the wrecking of rushes, bending, not breaking
Through an eon of tinkering; wiry in their resolution
Ghosting over furling meadow
Drowning out the night drone hedges
The battered town scoured clean.

Now the eight minute light's well spent
The world we were in, dissolved into
New; black and shroud in possibilities
Its happenings, all up in a gull shrill sky
In darkness, sacking till sun's resurrection
But for now until we feel its gaping yawn
We have artificial light.

Francis Curran

The Journey

She went down to the country
Snow was putting a blanket
On the high ground
She would not return
Alone
Naked winter trees
Witches in the half-light of evening
Observed him walking
Where there is only the traffic of thought
She would not return
Light, electric
Dragged his eyes from the darkening sky
And detail usurped reality.

Patrick Daly

Departure Lounge

Immaculately manicured nails curl around
The glossy, opulent pages of Elle or Cosmo,
She wears a smoky velvet choker at her throat,
Cartier gold and heavy Poison perfume, duty-free,
She roams the cat-walks of Milan, and in her reverie
Trails mink, thinks that crocodiles were designed
To ornament her handbags and stiletto shoes.
But I have read enough of shallow aspirations.
I will leave her mind
And trawl elsewhere along the row.

Short, military hair, sun-bleached blond,
Burnt thin on young, yet oddly weather-beaten skin.
Tight and lean he leans forward to unzip
A nylon webbing sack, blue on black,
Down-hill racer, mountain bikes, restless pages flipped
By fingertips with broken, black and oil-stained nails.
He leaves me breathless, careering Himalayan mountain tracks,
Yak and packhorse trails.
I will give his visions back
And move along the row.

Here is one! Stop here and enter in.
Middle-aged and spreading,
Polyester trousers shiny, wearing thin,
Straining at their nylon zip.
Over-riding colours brown and grey
Except for socks of not-so-subtle blue
To match his present thoughts.
Tabloid clutched at page three, knuckles white,
He chases nut-brown girls into the shelving, turquoise sea.
I do not wish to wait and see if he can catch one
Before I leave to catch my outward flight,
13.30 hours now boarding at Gate twenty-three.

John Tirebuck

Wee Boy

Carried within her being
She gave you life,
Letting you go in tears
And anguish,
Wrapped like a message
Against the dark,
Crying in your nakedness
And need
To catch the ear of strolling
Strangers.
Lifted by arms of care
And compassion,
Given a name in recognition
Of belonging,
Gary Holyrood you are special,
A survivor,
Welcome to the human family.

Shirley Johnson

4am

The sunlight's stopped behaving.
Laughing echoes up the long corridor.
The clock tower says four, again.
I sneak out the side door
The nurses forgot to lock,
And the sunshine starts up, for the last time.
I walk sideways, invisible,
As the clock tower follows,
Sieving the truth from delusions.

Angel Hart

Johnnie

I was introduced to Johnnie,
An early Christmas present,
For Joan, a lively ten-year-old,
Johnnie was less than a year old.

He was full of life and frisky,
Coming from a breed of palomino,
His mother had died so he became an orphan,
But her loss he soon overcame.

He was the central attraction
For Joan, her friends and her sisters,
Who could blame them for all the fuss?
With his big eyes so hypnotic.

He cast a spell on all, with just a look,
From nose to tail he was so appealing,
Johnnie being so young was unable to be ridden,
Time would take care of his growing.

Johnnie was a picture of health,
His colouring out of this world,
After he changed his winter coat,
He was spectacularly handsome and stylish.

Johnnie was poetry in motion,
He galloped round and round and up and down,
His golden body shimmering like corn,
His mane, golden blonde, like a banner waving.

This is natural beauty on the hoof,
By now Joan's time of waiting was over,
When she sits on his back Indian style,
The pair fly through the air without effort,
The bond between them is unique,
They move as one, what could be more natural?

Mary Lawson

On Millais' The Blind Girl

The sun is shining on your placid face,
Upturned to feel its beneficent rays,
The storm has passed in deepest indigo
But left its trace,
In wet folds of your shawl,
And distant rainbow, seal of Heaven's grace.

Dark and light are actual and implied,
In iridescent fields with sable crows,
Alive in sunlit hedge and shadow cast,
In little guide:
Betrayed with hands' tight clasp
Of love, that throws your sightless fear outside.

A humble instrument sweet music brings
To fine tuned ears, which consolation lights
A darkened world: as glowing butterfly
That jewelled clings
To your dull garb. Who knows?
Perhaps you heard the whisper of its wings.

Elinor Wilson

A Hauf Punna Mince, A La Burns

Gang ye ben the hoose, ma bonnie braw McDonal
an tak the pipey man wi ye, anaw anaw,
fur wi' the skirl o' th' pipes, yir blude'll be racin'
an it'll gie ye a boost,
as ye toil awaw.

Ho laddy! b'sure an' set the gas, unner the griddle,
at a ripe wee peep fur a fine middlin' sizzle
then we'll get heat fur the meat
an' the rid Spanish ingins,
so they kin dance an' jiggle,
ye ken, ye ken.

Next saut an' pepper the flesh, tae bring oot the flavour,
add a han'fu o' herbs, it's wur stumucks saviour
then ye kin boast most emphatically
that ye've definitely got a winner,
why it'll be the grandest meatmunchie in the land,
goad, wull we ever see its like again.

Weel noo, we've come to the end an' ah kin say more,
cos ah've ran oota words, that's a fact,
aboot *that* colossal hauf punna mince,
fur yir belly.

Archie Hardie

Millennium Dream

A cardboard box no longer home
Drug-crazed violence off the street
No orphan children rubbish comb
In ragged clothes, with blood-stained feet

Hunger pangs forgotten now
Brother share with brother
No barren soil beneath the plough
Infants suckle broody mother

No man entombed in prison cell
Crime exists no more
Each fortress now an empty shell
Virtue the ever open door

Eternal peace cease savage war
No flower of youth cut down
Mankind obeying nature's law
On bloody death all men shall frown

The Hiroshima cloud was cast
Man's destructive force completed
Remain a memory of the past
Embrace now the once defeated

Millennium beckons hope-filled heart
As one with friend and foe
On life's stage each man his part
The seeds of love to sow.

Thelma Thomas

My Broken Dreams

I was so full of fun laughter and joy,
I cycled down hills through country lanes
Walked with my loved one over daisies
Oh how happy was I, the breeze on my face.

I packed my case for the holiday we'd planned
My favourite place being Sicily
Up Mount Etna we climb so high
Sulphur bubbling from the crater.

My home - my garden was my life
Planting shrubs and flowers,
The fragrant smells of lilies and roses
I talked to them all each day.

I painted pictures - now on the wall,
I'd bake cakes, cook meals, make jam,
My days were full - so much I'd do,
Hobbies I had many.

Suddenly my world changed -
A new hip I had, but that went wrong -
Pain I've endured, but more was to come,
An artificial knee was next, pain unbearable.

I walked on crutches, yearning to be free,
Eight years passed - still the same.
One fatal day came while out shopping
Just as I was able to use one crutch.

Both legs are crippled, pain intense
I stare at my garden, plant flowers with my eyes
My bike just lies inside the shed
I take a deep breath and the tears just fall down.

Rosina Drury

Clouds In The Sky

Clouds in the sky,
Like wings of passing angels,
Shrouding God's glory, lest too bright it prove
For mortals
Yet take heart for He is watching,
This world is still His world and He is love.

Clouds in the mind
We stare and see no reason,
No purpose in the progress of the years,
Yet God is there, the Lord of every season
To banish all our doubts and needless fears.

Clouds in our eyes -
Like mist above the ocean,
We only see the gloom and miss the gleam,
The silver lining of the spirit's blessing
That cures our blindness in its healing stream.

Clouds in the sky
Look up for they are passing
And we shall see the splendour of the day,
If we can bear the light of God's own presence
Silent with wonder, we shall kneel and pray.

Mary Graves

So Much Still To Do

Never before in my life did I feel so loved
You taught me the meaning of love
Everything you did for me every day of our lives together
Was done because you loved me
And I loved you so very much, you were my whole life
Now all I feel is empty, numb and scared
Taken from me in an instant
Even all the love in my heart could not save you
I would give anything to have you back
We had so many years ahead of us, so much still to do
Our unborn children will never know how beautiful their mother was
And we can never give them all we never had
I know I will never again find what we had together, I don't even want to
They say love hurts and now I understand, I've never felt pain like this
The pain of living without you, never holding you again
I'm scared; it seems too much to bear my heart is broken into tiny pieces
It was held together by your love, you filled me up, made me complete
My only wish is that now you are in no more pain
I will carry your memory, your love and what we shared together
Around in my heart until it beats no more
And we are reunited again . . .
Sleep well my love.

Jacqui Watson

The Sculptor Of The Desert

The wind . . . the sculptor of the desert
Passed me by. Leaving a rippled pattern
In the sands of time.
Upward he sped, majestic dune,
Sending fine sprays of golden sand
Like fringes 'gainst a clear blue sky.
Cresting the ridge . . . he turned,
Spilling sand downwards.
Gathering speed . . . they stung my eyes and skin.
Singing and whispering as they passed
Of scorching sun and interminable heat.

Elwynne

Touch Me

Touch me. I am old
Worn out autumnskin
My sunken body still craves for
Something half-remembered.
Closeness of human warmth
Filling my emptyquiet
No kisses now only
Tightcold lips
Traditionally for a second from
Tightcold family of strangers
No kisses now only
Strongcold hands lifting me in this
Whitewalled eversmiling place
Touch me. I am old. I remember
Tenderthroated lovers who
Sighed in my neck
Warmwelded me close. I remember
Arms tight to quiet shaking sobs to security
Children holdswinging
No children now only
Controlled faces only
Appropriate
Exposure of emotion
Touch me. I am old. No womb now only
Whitecold echoes riding my days and the
Smiling of these uniforms
Kindly bringing the midmorning cup
Appeasing their guilt and
Hating my
Saliva gums.

Moyra Summers

They're Burning People Down At The Gasworks

Blackpool Central, excursion Platform Three.
The night sky was starless and widow black
A wind created dust devils across the deserted station.
The announcer spoke with the characteristic BR twang -
Some of the words were comprehensible -
'. . . last train delayed . . . fog on the Fylde . . .'
'The fog on the Fylde is all mine, all mine,' I mused.
Idly, I watched as a man appeared on Platform Four.
He was shambling sideways with a shuffling gait
And paused at each litter bin to rummage through the contents -
Like a bird searching for insects in a pile of leaves.
He carried a jaundiced bag bearing the Netto logo.
And wore a pair of antique jeans and trainers -
Topped off by an overcoat and a baseball cap.
I could see stubble protruding from his chin -
Like the bristles of an old toothbrush.
Oh no, I thought, *I hope he doesn't come this way.*
But he did, they always do, don't they . . . ?
In his eyes, I saw the labyrinthine depths of a mind in conflict.
I couldn't meet his gaze and made to turn away.
He leaned towards me and said, conspiratorially,
'They're burning people down at the gasworks!'
I inhaled deeply and there was indeed -
The barely perceptible stench of burning flesh on the breeze.

James E Cragg

My Gift

Oh rose,
Your beauty shouts forth
With formation so unblemished
And texture as silk.
Your fragrant scent
Captivates my senses,
Stirs my emotions,
Intoxicates my mind.
Oh, God, how grateful
I am for my perfect rose.
The silkiness of your sweet petals
As I brush you across my cheek,
Cools and tickles my skin.
I feel aroused
Romance fills my mind
Heart skips a beat
As I see the one
Who gave you to me
My gift, my rose.

Julianne Clarke

Beauty Is Elusive

(Written in 1977 in celebration of the Silver Jubilee of Queen Elizabeth II)

Beauty is elusive:
It pulses through our lives unrealised.
It might be in the flash of loving eyes
across a room of mixed acquaintances,
or in the grip of friendship's hand in trouble,
dust on wings of a bewildered butterfly,
or myriad prismatic colours in a drop of dew.

Spring warmth unveils velvet and satin petals
of grass-tucked primroses and celandines.
Unless we seek with child-like curiosity,
these hidden beauties do not flaunt themselves.

A skyward glance through lacy, leafy patterns
reveals what humble birds see all day long.
Stare, wonder, gaze at details new and marvellous!
Look fully down into the dog-rose depths -
behold the secrets hidden in its heart.

Consider forms of moss on ancient walls
crossing and dividing England's fields.
It is the little things we miss
by travelling too fast, not ponderously.

For inner restoration and tranquillity,
we need recourse to simpler things and ways -
basic joys, scents, colours, sounds and scenes
which are all there, if only we will see.

Stately beauty stands in swans' strong feathers,
dignified as our gracious Queen, whose birds they are.
Those happy ensigns which from roofs will flutter
this special year, have a historic
and untenable beauty of their own,
linking the changeless, ever-changing countryside
with day's delights, and beauty everywhere.

J M Gardener

American Ayr

We crossed the Brooklyn Bridge,
Heading north,
Toward bunker,
Giving thanks for pilgrims
And New England colour.

When seeing picket fences
And monuments
We saluted
On hallowed ground,

Then natives,
Negros
And Caucasians
All,

Stretched their wings,
West,
Over dust bowl 'n' prairie,
Feeding this infant nation,
Leaving lives behind,
Of colour,
There
With Liberty's bell,
By pony and wire,
Pony and wire,

Telling ancient canyons
And rivers that ran,
Of your stories drawn,
Sending cartoonists fingering hands,
Shooting stars into space,
Comic like,

And it was then and only then we rested,
Through winter snows,
For crossing over,
Coast to coast,
For reaching,
Our Californian gold,
In the year of '49. '49.

Andrew Fry

We Never Learn

We never learn, we pack them off
Young men wrapped tight in khaki cloth
They kiss their wives, they wave goodbye
And never hear their children cry
We bid them die for our belief
But for that death show little grief
Our tolerant and civil state
Gives way once more to rant and hate
We feel aggrieved and justify
Why flowers of youth must fight and die
We weep mock tears and shake our heads
When khaki hope returns in shreds
And bury neat in white crossed rows
The slaughtered lives who fought false foes.

We swear an end to war each time
And lay our wreaths at marble shrines
But history's hindsight, rich in years
Cannot dispel irrational fears
And men who seek to crown themselves
Will weave dissent until it swells
And causes tides to sail once more
Our soon scythed harvest off to war.

Jacqui Dunne

Winter Fantasy

When last I saw her naked in the breeze,
From winds and rain she stood with no defence.
Then barren, she was lacking confidence
With little solace there among the trees.

This winter morning brings another world,
Now dressed in white she glows in bridal-gown.
With falling snow, confetti cascades down
Amid the winter's glory now unfurled.

How proud she looks! I watch her with a sigh,
Outshining all those near and feel as though
Today a prima Donna she's been cast.

The image she projects no longer shy,
Overtly now her dress to all she'll show,
Before snow melts and leaves this tree unmasked.

Joan Zambelli

Go To Hell!

No one loves a scoundrel
A vagabond or a villain
For every robbing cowboy
There's always a sheriff Dillon.
It's the good against the bad guys
The Heaven against the Hell
That ever immovable object
And the irresistible force to tell.
Life would be so much different
If everyone knew right from wrong
But there'd be little space in Heaven
If the whole of mankind came along.
So continue your life of criminality
Keep ignoring the laws that be
Then you will surely meet the Devil
Leaving room up above for me!

John Topham

Portrait

'Now petal, come, drink up your tea,'
He shakes his head, turning away.
Lets fall his drawing of a girl,
Writhing black serpents intertwined.

Abstract paintings of every hue,
Critics acclaim him, artists too.
Solitary portrait 'not for sale' -
Fresh-faced girl, aflame with desire.

The crooked smile, the rakish cap,
A girl may dream of ravishment
After whispering words of love,
He leaves her to her innocence.

Marjorie Beaven

Am I Too Sensitive To Live

I am too sensitive
to mix my skin with others
It grates

I am too sensitive
to mix my breath with others
It strangulates

I am too sensitive
to mix my blood with others
It coagulates

I am too sensitive
to mix my heart with others
It intoxicates

I am too sensitive
to mix my mind with others
It infiltrates

I am too sensitive
to mix my soul with others
It contaminates

Am I too sensitive to live

Ursula Bayer

The Puppy

The puppy,
Chewing almost anything.
Sweet, cuddly and soft.
The size of fully grown rats.
Like an affectionate toy,
Making me happy when I am near,
Feeling as if I am an angel.
The puppy
Makes me feel so happy.

Georgina Swallow

The Child Inside

The woman who carries
The child inside
Your emotions will slowly
Pull you apart
What man alive today
Could ever understand
What goes on within
The woman who carries
The child inside
From a woman to a mother
Your child will always be
The most important prized possession
The world will ever see
So it's you
For this new gift of life
You are the woman
Who carries the child inside.

David Shepherd

Future

The future is actually very bright.
On the other side of the crisis, that is!
There are rendezvous points in history
Where all the birds come home to roost
Past wrongs and good deeds too
Consequences grown tall
Arrive from all quarters;
For a public convention and confrontation
As if by some unspoken agreement.
Something like that happened in Rome
And they didn't make it.
And the same in our day
Only on a higher scale.
If we can all make the leap
Resolve the issues fairly now.
If the powerful become wise
And the downtrodden wiser still
And hold the children's future in trust.
The future is actually very bright
On the other side of the crisis, that is!

John Cox

Vision

Man with a vision,
Give everyone a chance,
No matter what country, class or creed they belong.
Many topics to choose from.
A world of poetry never seen before in this country,
New works read by many.
Happiness given to thousands;
Verse expressed in different ways.
Poetry connecting the young and old,
Recording good and bad times, humour and sadness.
Capturing life and placing it in a printed form.
Male and female authors making their mark in time.

Gerald Snook

Time

What is time; time is something we all need -
Time to do this, time to do that -
But there is never enough time to do the things we need to do.
Time is precious there are times when we look forward
Times when we look back.
The happy times, the sad, the future and the past.
One thing is for certain, we cannot turn the clock back.

We can look to the future and hope it will be good,
But we never know what's round the corner.

There is a thing called fate and an open gate.
There are many roads to travel when you get through that gate
And some of us make the wrong decision when we go through.
I hope you choose the right road and hold your head up high,
Don't look up and don't look down and one day you will
wear a crown.

If you put yourself on a pedestal you can make that golden rule
Will I be good or will I be bad, will I be happy or will I be sad?
Anyway, whatever you choose I hope the world is good to you.
Just remember to get on that pedestal then you can
always look back.
The future is what you make it but you cannot change your past.
Time goes on and on and on . . .

Yvonne Cooper

The Other Love!

What is that other love we talk about?

Forbidden love!

We don't understand
Woman and woman
Man and man.

Lovers meet in smoky places
Kiss and dance in long embraces!
Strangers when they meet and when they go.
Secrets we don't know.

Passions of the night.

Woman and woman
Man and man
No wrong or right.

Lovers meet in smoky places.
Kiss and dance with painted faces.
Strangers when they meet and when they go!
Secrets we don't know.

Passions of the night.

Woman and woman.
Man and man
No wrong or right.

Pamela Hanover

Mercutio

And still you spoke
of nothing

and your thoughts so often
passed us by -

for a dream of love you borrowed
Cupid's wings

and Queen Mab's chariot
to draw your words

in the likeness of a sigh . . .

How could your gallant spirit
die?

when a single prayer from your
idle brain

would make us all believe -

my friend you left with
no goodbye

and how I mourn your mischievous rhyme

for what is life without our
dreams?

and we all know, that dreamers
never lie . . .

Steve Gunning

If You Weren't There . . .

If You weren't there God in my life,
I would be an ever empty vessel,
Sailing on an ever stormy sea.

You love me unconditionally,
Never scolding or chastising,
You trust Your child will retain
The wisdom of yesteryears.

The spiritual path can be testing,
To make sure I stay on course,
But the beauty of knowing You,
And the feeling that I'm safe
Far exceeds the problems that life can sometimes make.

Your child is ever grateful,
For everything I receive,
I learn to make decisions,
Based on love and guidance received,
I love You with an open heart,
And trust the path I tread,
For You and the angels are guiding lights.

I have too my inner voice,
Knowing this is the one I must follow.
It's not always the easy one,
So I am grateful Lord, You are in my life.
My vessel is a full one,
Full of love and gratitude,
For having You in my life.

Catherine M Simpson

Residue

(In the home of a spinster aunt - recently deceased)

Here is something left of a hidden hopelessness,
Desperation turned to an acceptance of fate,
Kismet, Hardy, that sort of thing.
Elegiac motes, adrift in the air, reflect
The passing of a stoicism lost on today's generation:
Pain behind an embroidered fire-screen
Armoured by spinsterish clothes,
Rules, social mores,
Scars hardly to be seen,
Hiding a secret not to be disclosed at any cost?
Here a plea was left off
That formerly moved closer to some kind of ending,
Toward a finally wished for and faintly whispered
Amen.

Richard Unwin

Ode To My Nieces, Sonia And Anna

Oh, baby darlings, both under two years of age,
You bring out the best avuncular qualities within me
On the rare occasions that we meet!
Toddler Sonia, fair, ruddy-complexioned, light brown-eyed
Framed with thin, brown hair.
A spitting miniature image of my brother-in-law.
As you take your first, faltering steps,
Your inquisitiveness knows no bounds
As your new-found freedom tears the shackles
That kept you curtailed to your cot,
A fiery, Taurean personality in nascent form can be seen
Imprinted in the shards of future time . . .
You will make your mark on the future,
This I can guarantee by observing your behaviour . . .
To sweet, beautiful month-old Anna with sharp facial features,
Clear-cut eyes and nose.
It is clear that you will be a future heart breaker!
Although you lie helpless, fragile, doll-like
And totally dependent in your crib,
Relying on your parents for your basic needs,
As you look with your guileless, intelligent sepia eyes into my eyes,
Brows furrowed with intense concentration,
Framed within your square face
With thick curly locks of dark brown hair,
Whilst strongly clutching my index finger with your puny hand,
I feel a new, revelatory emotion
To guard, protect and nurture you
From the evils in this insane world!
When the two of you are near me,
The invisible bonds of kinship wrought in our blood and DNA,
Awaken within me not only the duties that kinship brings,
But also the duties that we owe to others as decent human beings!

Robin Halder

A Day Out

You look around at people and wonder what they have been?
What have they achieved in life, and just what have they seen?
He! may have been a doctor, a lawyer, accountant,
Or the driver of a bus
She! may have been an air-hostess, a bank clerk or maybe a nurse,
A shop assistant maybe,
Might even have sold you a purse!

As they sit in the tearooms it's time for a snack,
Maybe a scone and some tea,
Some quiet reflection with friends, have a chat.
Make plans for the future now retirement is here,
Take up a hobby or go on a cruise!
Look after the grandchildren, catch up with the news!

Then browse around the department store,
A special outfit to find
A wedding, a christening, or a grandchild's twenty-first!
Or any other celebration it has to be just the right kind!

Then head to the car park of bus stop,
Go home to their own little world,
Then try on the outfit in comfort
To make sure it's the right one for her.

A partner no longer to share with,
When all she needs him to say, is
'You're looking well there girl!'
And, 'Did you have a nice day?'

Gwyneth A Llewellyn Rea

Touch

The touch on the skin is such a live sensation
A wave of pleasure that flows along a sensual pathway.
Stroking, caressing, softly embracing -
The feel of another person's closeness.
The warmth that flows from one who touches to another -
Send deep spasms of delight to the sensory tingling flesh.
Pressing hands on warm responsive skin -
Gives pleasurable awareness of ecstasy.
Stroking, massaging - stimulating blood flow for a rosy glow.
Gently soothing tension away from stiffening limbs.
Easing painful joints by warm embrace.
The power of touch sends messages,
Where words cannot penetrate.
The closeness and intimacy, when two bodies meet,
Bring magical stimulation from head to the feet.
The feel of skin - so soft and supple.
Silky, and like velvet on a newborn calf.
The softness of a baby's skin -
Delicate, and like peaches and cream.
To touch another, is to give a signal of communication.
That loving touch between a baby and its mother.
To touch with love is to experience a sensual pleasure -
Like no other.
Oh, please touch me forever!

Helen Sarfas

How Do I Move On?

If you could have seen inside my heart
You would have seen my love for you

You would have seen
How much I cared

You would have seen
The tears I cried
When you were ill
And I didn't know what to do

You would have seen
The pride and joy
When we walked down the street
Holding hands
Joking, laughing and talking

You would have seen
The times I prayed to God
To thank Him for choosing you
To be a part of my life

You would have seen
How distraught I was
When someone used, abused and hurt you

And finally
You would have seen
How you have broken it
And the pain you have caused
That just won't go away
Then maybe
Just maybe
You could answer one question for me
How do I move on?

Pauline E Reynolds

What Is Love?

Love is that indefinable thing that makes mankind unique.
The inspiration that makes a man offer his life for another,
The feeling that can make a man ecstatically happy,
Or sick with fear for someone else's welfare,
Indeed, love is a dish with many recipes,
As diverse a menu, as ever reached a table in the feast of life,
It is that glow that makes a rainy day seem warm,
And gives welcome to a stranger in a thunderstorm,
It is the oil that calms the troubled waters when two lovers
can't agree,
And paints over the cracks in a friendship so that others cannot see.
It makes the ugly beautiful; the days go by quickly,
A pretty girl that is in love will lose her vanity.
The love of a mother for her newborn child,
must bring tears of joy,
She cares not about its wrinkles, or whether a girl or boy.
The love of a man for a woman, or a woman for a man,
This child that is born of love,
Gives pleasure like nothing else on Earth can.
So . . . what is love but life at its grandest,
A God given gift to man.

Daniel P Callaghan

Risen

I saw Him, as if for the first time,
As I looked up to Him, His voice
re-sounding,

'Mary,' He said.

Recognition was mine
in an instant.
'Master!'

My Lord
was risen!

Sharon Elton

The Sorrow Of Love

It is like the twilight when it embraces a dazed dreaming,
This breath is called by her onto vibrating webs of silk,
The poet is caught and cries with the song of love's night,
Aphrodite's voice resounds through a labyrinth of echoes,
Which shatters those glass hearts, we lie in crystal slithers
Which cut into
Dawn's vision,
Our consciousness is rising like a lost chant from Heaven.

The fallen angels are cast into Hades which is beckoning
The descent
Into flames.

We
Spiral through a maze of corridors, those broken mirrors
Which are like
The sorrow of love which haunts the rising morning dew.

N S Pearce

Winter

I love winter's cold,
Dark nights with curtains drawn,
A warm room, cosy, comforting,
Sparkling webs at dawn.
Walking on chilly snowy days,
Crunching through frosty leaves,
Winter sunsets,
Snowy eaves.
Trees lacy boughs
Against a sky of grey,
Frosty windows,
A snowy day,
A holly bush
With leaves dark green
And scarlet berries in between.
An early snowdrop
Pushing into view,
All shared with you.

Sybil R Collins

Freedom

To be able to choose between this and that,
Deciding to go or to stay,
That's freedom of choice.

To expound on politics, music and such,
To criticise, or to praise,
That's freedom of voice.

There's freedom in movement of body and limb,
For those not afflicted with pain
Or some crippling disease.

There's a freedom in watching a bird on the wing,
Or closing your eyes to the rain,
No blind man has these.

Of all of the freedoms, the greatest to me,
Is God's gift of an active mind,
That's freedom of thought.

No matter what freedoms are taken away,
By others with power or wealth,
This one cannot be bought . . .

Joan Hammond

Famine, Hunger, Starvation

Who can say in all honesty that they
Have not witnessed, by the sight of their
Own eyes, on television, the slow death of
People by starvation, can they say, as they
Watched the pictures on TV, of children and
Babes in arms, their last moments of life,
The flickering eyes before they closed forever,
That they were preoccupied and really did not
Notice those people on TV.
The people dying of starvation, are subjected to
A kind of ostracism or, in a European sense,
Beyond the pale, because they do not belong
To the human race, or so the inhabitants
Of first world countries think, the majority of
That world never once in their lives experienced,
Any kind of starvation, particularly of the belly kind,
Their only experience of hunger was 'supper-time hungry'
They are disgusted that people should allow
Themselves to sink to such a level!

Gerard Kenny

A Rare Day

How we embraced
All those green fields.
We grew bold as buttercups
Holding the sun in our arms.

Excitement stirred the moors
And peace crept up
From all that grew
On the wild slopes,

And we, so folded into the earth
And soaked with sun,
Were confused to find
Our feet instead of roots.

Elsie Hamilton

The Ageing River

In the beginning I was a stream,
Trickling over rocks and spouts of grass
Through spaces between trees,
From the baby spring to the mother ocean.

Over the years wisdom has filled me,
Deepening my bed and increasing my breadth.
I have seen trees grow, bloom and fade,
I have watched men fight with hands, swords and guns.

Grass, trees and shrubs diminished,
Wooden foot bridges grown to cross my strength.
From the pretty shade of trees,
Where rabbits play and my babble may be heard.

I have moved to a concrete field,
Where metal monsters roar and scream
Clouding the air with thick and sticky poison.
From the time men came with mechanical swords
To make the trees scream.

I am drowned out now,
My course has never altered,
And yet I find myself in some place new.

Samantha Douglas

Growing Up

My friends at school were a lively gang
'From the rough estate,' Mum would say
We'd talk girlie stuff about boys we liked
And who we thought was gay.

Then most of my friends, me excluded
Started to grow at an alarming pace,
They developed curves and needed bras
I developed spots on my face.

As they blossomed into young shapely girls
I'd stare in the bedroom mirror
And look at my pimples and greasy hair
And wish that I could be slimmer.

And then came the curse that affected all women
A drag at the very best
But there was a benefit - I'd get out of swimming
And watch in my pants and vest.

Jo Sinfield

Golden Days

A nip in the morning air
Early swirls of mist in the valley
Harvest almost in
Bales scattered on sun-kissed stubbles

On such a glorious, golden day
You entered the world
Ten tiny fingers, ten tiny toes
And a shock of dark hair

Johnston birthmark at nape of neck
We rolled you over just to check!

Proud dad recalls on every birthday
Homebound from hospital - a golden Strathmore valley
Rejoicing in our baby girl
While grieving for a grandad never met

Cosy and snug in our York House nest
Great Granny Murray comes to inspect,
'My, what a braw leg that bairn has'
Mum sheds a tear - hormones a mess!

Lazy, hazy September days
Stretch on into an Indian summer

Only remember one 5th of September
Not warm and mellow like the first
In twenty years of golden memories -
A rainy second birthday in a string of sunny parties

Sun-kissed stubbles strewn with bales
On such a glorious, golden day
Our beautiful, darling daughter
Amy Frances was born

Twenty years on and September holds promise
Of an Indian summer again . . .

Irene Johnston

The Book Sale

I am drawn inside by the cheap sign,
Nodding to the lady busy at her desk,
Who peers over glasses precariously perched.
I stroll through cluttered sections,
Which display such a range of mediocrity,
And so little which seems of any interest.
Yet I love the smell of ageing print;
Fading edges of pages, brittle to touch,
Singed almost like toast;
Garish paperbacks generously creased,
With lurid 1970s fonts;
Old history tomes of unfashionable views,
With annoyingly illegible margin notes -
All strangely de rigueur.
As ever I leave with nothing in hand,
Yet glad that such simple things
Still find a place in the world.

David Francis Barker

Eurythmics Jinx

Walking on broken glass,
Glass in the bedroom,
Mirrors the relationship:
Haven-cum-minefield.

Do I want you to find this?
So much guilt-inflicting power,
Yet impotent to make you change.

'Cruisin' for a bruisin''
Using and abusing,
All of us lose,
And never stop to muse,
That violence never woos.

Intergenerational transmission
Of force that doesn't listen.
Taking up our parental positions,
And lacking liberating vision.

The road of no return,
Innocence lost along the way,
Too ingrained to unlearn,
Torn apart and ready to fray.

Unknowingly did we discern
Each other in order to make *them* pay?
Surely someone else's turn,
How it started . . . unfair to say.

A rage that's too repressed to burn,
Best forgotten come what may.
It is peace for which we yearn,
That tomorrow be a real new day.

Cheryl Livesey

Caroline

Your arm holds me tight
You touch my cheek with yours
Love from out of my heart pours
My heart beats so quick
Your love my deepest desire
Your lovely lips so divine
Wonderful when they meet mine
A kiss of love so sweet
We shudder from our head to our feet
A love comes here to keep
Flows like a river so deep
Till we go to sleep
Sweet dreams of love
You are like Heaven above
A burning fire full of love
Dawn breaks on a lovely day
Your light shines that way
A touch so sweet every day
Your love is mine tonight
As our love burns so bright.

Gordon Forbes

To Be A Poet

To be a poet
I have to be
To write my poem
For you and me
Happy poems, sad poems
I will write them all
For the people's pleasure
Enjoy them all
And when I am dead
They will remember me
Through my poems
For you and me.

Greeny

Alone With Footy

I am so alone, want to go back home,
Don't you all agree?
You know I was that tomboy sitting in that tree
I was seven, never to be,
To be me, a child, a child oh so wild,
With my hair running free,
But sitting there without a care, so revered,
Why? I thought at the time
I really wanted to be me, to score and much more
To reach every core and see
All the normality and much more to me
It is my baby, to sit down and be a clown
And know we are the maybe.

Daniel Deaves

The Lefts Of Man

In evening's conversation with a modern maid
The other night, the subject strayed
From verse to acting, prose to plays
And I discovered in these days

The reason for the sometimes quite excessive zeal
Which I have noted in the female sex: they seem to feel
Theirs is the right, the role, the duty now to call the shot,
Decide the course; declare what should be and what not

Describing this reforming action as evolution, not reaction
Not for them (or some, I should be fair) an equal task
To face with partner problems of career or passion
No, they grasp society irrespective of propriety; they ask

No quarter, give no mercy, take a man and wring him dry
And no compassion wets their eye . . .
It's true, that modern man's no longer quite fulfilled
With pirate passion, trampling over foes he's killed

Though tough in business, stern in war
And still he'll even up the score
But 'tis the dreamers of our sex who always have defied the hex
Of ignorance and folly: mightier than the sword the word

And what is spoken, written, cast in air will change forever
When Martin Luther King spoke of his dream, the world took fire!
And women do this too . . . but I have a little fear
That in newfound freedom - their natural desire

To shine alone might lead some down that sorry path
Which so many men have trod. There is room
Both for the dreamer and the doer, if at the hearth
Or business, and when from cradle to the tomb

Both man and women share the joys and chores
No 'this is mine' and 'that is yours'
Together, striving, fighting, loving to their goal
Then we shall have a world that's whole.

Geoffrey Speechly

School Years

Off to school,
Answer education's calls.
Build towards our futures,
Avoid easy falls.
Friends by our sides,
The best times of our life.
Working together,
No worry or strife.
Then the end of the year,
The exams begin
Those who've worked hard,
Are certain to win.
The challenge of a lifetime,
School may sometimes seem.
But with a little hard work,
It can turn out a dream.

Katie Turner

Regret

I warm my hands by your fire
Stretching my legs and uncurling my toes
The room has a presence, a feeling of desire
Which gives a strange shiver from my neck to my nose

I wait for your company
But you're biding your time
I lay back and relax
Whilst the moment is mine

Thoughts of odd things
Wander about my mind
No answers, but the questions
Are all I can find

Regret of that deed
That cannot be undone
So secret I cannot tell her
Or tell anyone

But sit back, and relax
Whilst time is my friend
There's not long to go
Until it's the end

The room is so peaceful
But empty in her wake
Those bloodcurdling screams
That keep me awake

But relax now
What's done has been done
And cannot be changed . . .
By anyone

As my feet get too warm
And my mind fills with pain
I get up to walk
And leave the house again.

Ryan Smith

Revelation

A ray of sunshine, a beam of light,
A baby born in perfect sight,
Ten fingers, ten toes,
Two eyes, one nose,
So innocent, so pure,
New life, to be sure.

That evil that grips over those so young,
A story may wish to remain unsung,
Pain strikes the vulnerable,
Who aren't able to say,
The pain that runs through them day by day,
Thunder and lightning awash over the bay,
There's nothing left,
There is no strength but to pray,
And that illness that lies through Baby Girl,
That cold hand that grips her heart,
Her crying is shrill.

Mother holds Baby, curled up in her arms,
That Baby that's lost all her innocent charms,
Baby is shaking,
Life trickles away,
Mother has only three words left to say,
I love you
Is strong,
Their time together not long.

And as Baby lays lifeless against Mother's chest,
Mother's heart is breaking as she puts Baby to rest,
But in her heart of hearts
She's secretly glad,
That's Baby's pain is over,
There's no need to be sad.

She watches her Baby being put into the ground,
A tiny white coffin,
Not a more beautiful Baby,
Is ever to be found.

Carlyn Coyle

Inocente

(Dedicated to Jean Charles de Menezes)

Green, yellow, blue
Bang! Bang!
What the *'porcos'* did to you.
Just for riding on the tube.

Black. Black. Black.
Inside their hearts.
A foreign fitting means guilt.
The prejudice will never wilt.

Red. White. Blue.
Guns held shakily.
The Big L tries to keep face.
Like the Big Apple kept faith.

Yellow. Yellow. Yellow.
Are the bellies of the law.
Friendly fire shot in pure fear.
The face of justice, I sneer!

Why did you run young man of only twenty-seven?
You should be walking the streets of London,
Not locked up behind the gates of Heaven.

Sarah Parry

One Soul

There is a love that words cannot master
It defies expression by mere language
The communication of such a joining of souls
Can only ever be achieved
By gentle touch
Warm caress
Meeting of eyes
Understanding of hearts
Two lives surrendered
Each to the fulfilment
Of the other's dreams
Happiness, purpose, hope
For in such a consummation
There is no difference
And the hopes and dreams of two lives
Become the heartbeat of one.

Martin Collins

The Eagle

It's wonderful to see an eagle in flight,
Soaring upward till it's reached a great height.
It glides and swoops down on its prey,
A mouse is caught as it tries to get away.

It's such an impressive, majestic looking bird,
Strong and fearless, such a powerful bird.
It makes its nest in a cliff top high,
Where it flies from each day, high into the sky.

It goes out in search of food each day,
Some unsuspecting small creature is its prey.
With speed and accuracy it takes careful aim,
Its unfortunate victim to kill or main.

Yes, it's a beautiful sight to see an eagle in flight,
Soaring upward to a great height.
Up, up into the sky so high,
With its huge wings it can easily fly.

Richard W Cummings

A Sonnet For My Love

Touch is what binds us, what nurtures and finds us
Touch is the feeling of silky - soft skin -
Now I undress you, smooth and caress you,
Touch is an ecstasy starting within.

Start to arouse me, a feathersoft pressing,
Breathe in the scents that steal from within.
I love you to smell me, to push and compel me
To massage the juices that seep from my skin.

Stroking and kneading, caress every hollow -
Your touch is a magic with no recipe.
Tension that finds us, then loses, then binds us -
Minds are usurped in this fierce mystery.

Peace pounding through me - can love now begin?
Touch ends the battle that both of us win.

Lilian Perriman

Goodnight Vienna

It's barely fifteen minutes since I found his body there
Slouching on the settee with a vomit-induced stare
An empty prescription bottle sticking to his clammy hand
And half a dozen tablets scattered round like grains of sand
A crisp manila envelope sealed with little haste
'To whom it may concern' inscribed upon its face
As I stooped to pick it up, I swear he smiled at me
I knew, at last, he'd arrived upon the place he yearned to be.

The letter read:
'If you've found this note you're too late to say goodbye
If you're reading this then I've already left your life
If you're stood there wondering why I've done what I have done
The answer is life and all it brings, and, what I've left undone
Please pass on all my love to the girl I love the most
Tell her I'll watch over her with Father, Son and Holy Ghost
And one more thing - before you think that you can save my life
Is that everything I have I leave to the boys and my humbled wife.'

Now as I look down on his form I know I will not cry
I will not wince I will feel no pain, I will not question why
I will instead be happy that he is at peace at last
That his troubles and his worries are now all in the past
He often told me that he felt he was destined for greater things
That the life he had was difficult with all the hurt it brings
And I know now what he meant when said under his breath -
'Media vita in morte sumus' (in the middle of life we are in death.)

Paul Anthony Scott

The Meaning

The meaning of life now apparent
From all that I saw once before
For all that I see now of my life
Is the way to go forward with all

Before I can go I must see through
Seems my life has been mapped out for me
I no longer have any say in what happens
Just the way that things turn out to be

I'm happy to think now I will also
Be content in my future to agree
I feel a sensible kind thoughtful person
All my troubles have gone set me free

With all this behind me I need to
Get on with my life as it comes
And not dwell in my past thoughts existence
But go forward for the rest of my chums.

S C Matthews

T Beautiful Union

Life is just a moment and God knows nobody
Really cares.
I need to be alone when I suffer.
Where's the nearest cancer ward?

This is my ritual.
Take shoes off, put blue slippers on.
TV on, nightmare ends briefly.
It's my destiny to have fun with chicks but I'm
Cursed by sweet Mumsy.

Married to Mumsy and expressing her feelings.
It's my destiny to love someone.
It's Mick's destiny to go to charity shops.
It's my destiny, one day, to become famous.
It's Mumsy's destiny to go to church.

It's my destiny to die.

Alan Cornelius

The Simplicity Of Creativity

The genuine buzz, excitement and sanity
To provoke the subjects deemed too frivolous for society.
Questioning and pushing boundaries
To extract the truth from mad-capped adventures.
I love how one can have that wide-eyed attentiveness
A child does the first time Daddy shows them how
He effortlessly removes his thumb to the child's amusement.
The fact that you can sit there
And have that rare measure of insanity to confess
That you do not agree when the odds are stacked against you.
You cannot force or fake creative tendencies.
'Why would you sing Hallelujah if it means nothing to ya?'
One may be eccentric and a romantic idealist,
But I can assure that my dreams are far more fruitful and colourful.
Do not mock me for my dreams.
Dr King had a dream . . . and my best friend is white.

Shemelia Douglas

Death City

A summer's day, hot in the city,
Bustle and noise, people hurrying about
To catch the tube or a public bus,
Suddenly an explosion, so loud like thunder,
Everything stops, silent, listening,
Screams and shouts rend the air,
Dust, smoke, fumes everywhere.

The truth comes out, a bomb has hit,
Three more to follow, horror, fear, silent prayers,
The injured moan, mortal wounds inflicted,
Traumatised in shock, the dying groan,
This summer day, death has hit a city,
Not soldiers at war, only innocent folk,
Suicide bombers from a terrorist flock.

Elisabeth Hiddleston